GW00363503

love @ first site

How to find a relationship online

Susan Broom and Marc Zakian

love @ first site

How to find a relationship online

Susan Broom and Marc Zakian

Icon Books

Published in the UK in 2005
by Icon Books Ltd., The Old Dairy,
Brook Road, Thriplow, Cambridge SG8 7RG
email: info@iconbooks.co.uk
www.iconbooks.co.uk

Sold in the UK, Europe, South Africa
and Asia by Faber and Faber Ltd.,
3 Queen Square, London WC1N 3AU
or their agents

Distributed in the UK, Europe, South Africa
and Asia by TBS Ltd., Frating Distribution Centre,
Colchester Road, Frating Green, Colchester CO7 7DW

Published in Australia in 2005
by Allen & Unwin Pty. Ltd., PO Box 8500,
83 Alexander Street, Crows Nest, NSW 2065

Distributed in Canada by Penguin Books Canada,
90 Eglinton Avenue East, Suite 700,
Toronto, Ontario, M4P 2YE

ISBN 1 84046 677 4

Text copyright © 2005 Susan Broom and Marc Zakian

The authors have asserted their moral rights

No part of this book may be reproduced in any form, or by any means,
without prior permission in writing from the publisher.

Waiver: All of the information contained in this book is believed to be correct at the
time of going to press. The information in this book is provided for guidance purposes
only. Icon Books and its authors cannot be held responsible for any errors, omissions or
factual inaccuracies.

Special thanks to
Ben, David and Keith

Typesetting by Ann Buchan (Typesetters)
Printed and bound in the UK by Bookmarque Ltd

CONTENTS

ABOUT THE AUTHORS

Susan Broom became a freelance journalist after a long career in TV and was a regular contributor to the *Mail on Sunday* magazine, *Night and Day*. She is currently writing a novel about dating.

Marc Zakian is a writer and journalist who regularly contributes to the *Times*, the *Telegraph* and the *Guardian*. He has written for various other magazines and newspapers in the UK and abroad. Marc has also worked in TV as a scriptwriter and editor.

Marc and Susan met while internet dating. While love didn't blossom, the idea for this book did.

Safety

There are some basic rules of safety for internet dating. Many people – mostly women – are put off internet dating because of the potential dangers of coming into contact with anonymous strangers.

The obvious contradiction to this argument is that if you were going to harm somebody, you would not give them your photograph, email and mobile phone number which could all identify you. Internet dating is almost certainly safer than randomly meeting someone in a bar or a bus queue.

But there are some basic safety rules for dating:

1. Don't give anyone your home address until you're sure you can trust them. When giving out your geographical location, limit yourself to a wide area.
2. In the first instance, exchange only mobile phone numbers. Remember when you call people that your number will come up, unless you block it.
3. If you sense that somebody is lying – married when they say they are single – stop communication with them now.
4. Meet people in a public place, where there are other people around. On your first meeting, it is best to make your own way to and from the venue. It is best not to accept an offer of transport.
5. Keep others informed. Leave details of your meeting with family or friends when seeing a dater for the first time.
6. Trust your instincts – don't meet again if you have any doubts.

Chapter 1

INTERNET DATING

Romancing in the 21st Century

Once upon a time you married the boy or girl next door; now we barely know their name. Once upon a time there were match-makers, dating agencies, and newspaper personals. Now we like our food fast, our coffee instant, and our dates express via the internet.

We have embraced the cyber-love revolution with open arms. Internet dating is now an out-and-proud, 21st-century, world-wide phenomenon. It's the place where two out of three singletons search for love. The UK alone currently boasts over 800 dating sites, romancing 3 million people from every section of society – from overworked professionals, to silver-surfers, to single parents.

This book will help you get the best from the experience. If you are new to internet dating, it's a step-by-step guide to love online. If you are an old hand, it will help you improve your chances of finding a relationship. If you're not looking, it's an entertaining insight into the exciting, unpredictable and sometimes amusing world of cyber romance. And if you're a nervous novice – concerned that the net is populated by the sort of people you shy away from on the train – we'll show you how to internet date safely and easily.

Cute computers

For years the words computer and nerd were joined at the unhip. The world of hard drives and RAM had all the amorous appeal of a filing cabinet, and the clichéd view of someone behind a computer screen was grungy geek, not potential date.

But then the internet arrived, and the computer stepped out of the workplace and into the home. In the late 80s online dating was born in a wild and unique newsgroup called soc.singles – a pioneer band of singletons who saw the potential for the internet to bring people together.

Compuserve and AOL soon realised the internet's potential to create romance, and their dating forums were hugely popular. Instant messaging services like ICQ and MSN promoted hundreds of love matches, many of which are still going strong – with their children now discovering that mummy and daddy met on a computer screen.

ICQ

The granddaddy of instant messaging systems, ICQ – or 'I Seek You' – lets you chat in real time on your computer. It also has a members' search system, so you can look for people with similar interests, as well as a free singles section, where you can log the numbers of potential matches, then chat with them when they are online. www.icq.com

The dot.com boom cashed in on cyberdating's potential, and commercial sites burst onto the scene. The market is still growing, with one UK site currently claiming 2 million daters. Alongside this, specialist sites have appeared, and we will introduce you to the internet love of cowboys, brainiacs, bikers, cat fanciers and foot fetishists.

By the late 90s online dating was never out of the media. Journalists devoted reams of articles to telling us the fad was fun, but were always careful to mention that they themselves would never have to 'resort' to the internet to get a date. The stigma attached to computers – magnified by the boom in internet pornography – meant that online dating was like 1950s sex – everybody was doing it, but nobody talked about it.

In the last few years, however, internet dating has come out of the closet. Not before time when you think that 20-somethings – who have grown up with the internet – find it strange *not* to internet date; many 30-somethings are by now veteran internet daters, who have had several relationships via dating sites; 40-somethings, many of them coming out of long-term relationships, find online dating the quickest way to get back in the saddle; and silver-surfers are discovering the possibilities of love after 60.

Online dating is now so normal that there are offices where all the staff singletons sign up for one site, and gather round the water cooler to compare notes.

But internet dating is still only fifteen years old – and, like any teenager, it doesn't yet have fixed rules. This book will show you the best place to find the relationship you are looking for, stop you from wasting money and time, and guide you along the cyber highway of love.

Logging on

You need three things to join the internet dating revolution.

- Access to a computer. If you don't have a home PC, a local library or internet café will provide internet points.
- An email account. You can create free ones at hotmail.com or yahoo.com (go to www.hotmail.com or mail.yahoo.com and follow the instructions).
- And, if you are joining a site which charges, a credit card to pay for their services.

Chapter 2

THE LOVE MACHINE

A Guide to the Sites

There are over 800 UK dating sites, and thousands worldwide. For newcomers, it's like wandering into love's own department store. Each site offers hundreds of people looking for someone like you. Beguiled by the promise of this new-found romance, you sign up to the first one you visit.

And why not? The site says it's free. But a cyberdate is like lunch – there are no free ones. With a very few exceptions, you'll have to pay to make contact with fellow surfers. Once you do, you may discover that the site has only a tiny number of members – none of whom are right for you.

The internet is an excellent 'shop front': you can't tell who is behind the scenes – it could be a team of hardworking office cupids, or some bloke with a PC in an attic. Run a search for internet dating sites and you'll get 40,000 hits. Many are nothing but a link to another site – their way of earning money. And when you finally get there, the quality and suitability of the dating sites is unpredictable.

Fortunately, you bought this book. We have trawled the net, and spoken to the people who use and run the sites. This chapter will show you how to avoid wasting your time and money, and help you maximise the possibility of getting in touch with the right people. It will point you to well-run sites which provide a genuine service, and will flag up scams designed to take your money and run.

Free love

Free love died in the 1960s. With internet dating, 'free' actually means sites won't charge you to register – if you want to contact another member, you'll have to pay. As there is no known form of dating which doesn't involve making contact with somebody, *most* sites claiming to offer 'free dating' do not.

The good news is that some sites let you contact other members and exchange email/phone numbers without paying. Some limit the number of free contacts you can make to two or three a day. Sensibly, many newer sites don't charge until they have built up a large enough membership to offer a decent service.

There is nothing wrong with internet dating sites charging. They staff an office, check photographs and profiles and answer member queries. A good site costs money to run, and most charge a fraction of the fees of conventional dating agencies.

But when it comes to something as emotive as dating and love, people are easily conned. A dodgy dating website could be a nice earner so, as a prospective punter, make sure that a site has sufficient members to offer you a choice of potential partners. You wouldn't shop at a market where the fruit and veg weren't on show, so don't join a site where you can't see profiles and pictures before you part with your pounds.

Fees vary from £10 to £20 a month, with discounts offered if you sign up for three months or a year. Payment is by credit card. Watch out for sites which automatically renew your membership: you stop logging on, believing your membership has expired, when in fact they have charged you for another month. To stop them going shopping with your credit card, when you join, click on the billing section and cancel automatic renewal.

Choosing the right dating site is all about balancing quantity and quality. Some quantity is essential: there's more chance of pulling at a party with hundreds of people than at one with ten. As one dater put it, 'Small sites are like a goldfish bowl, you see the same old fish swimming round and round.' A start-up website needs time to build up its membership, so be very wary about joining a new set up if it's not free.

Before handing over your money, search the profiles and see if there is a good selection of members with the same kind of interests as you. If you want to see what people look like, scroll through the profiles to check out the form – some websites have more photos than others. Look for active members by checking when they last logged on – old profiles are kept online to bolster numbers. If a member has not been active for a month, they are probably no longer in the market for a relationship.

Most paying sites allow you to register, but until you pay your subscription you can't send or read messages. This means that your initial excitement at finding several people who are ideal dating material is dampened when you realise that they can't access your messages.

If money is no object, you can join every site on the net. Most of us don't have a spare £2,000 a month to pay for this, so strike a balance by joining one or two good paying sites as well as some free ones. If a site you join is not providing you with potential love-mates, don't give up – move on to the next one.

Smart surfing

Bear in mind too that cyberdaters sniff 'new blood' – which is why you receive lots of interest in the first few days of joining.

Sites encourage this by giving daters the option to run a search for new members.

A good strategy is to join a site for one month, make contact with people who interest you, then join a different site the following month. You may come across the same profiles as you move from site to site. If you join a large site, log in regularly and keep making new contacts, you can easily have one date a week. It's depressing to see this as a numbers game, but the saying about frog-kissing was never truer than in internet dating, because you will only find out if you have chemistry with someone after writing and speaking to them for a few weeks. In real life, you usually spark with someone first, then get to know them later.

To help create the sensation of real-life chemistry, most sites have special features to bring compatible members together – something of a relief when a site has 30,000 profiles. They match people by age and location. Location is important, as many sites are international. Love may know no boundaries, but a retired Lebanese lollipop lady and a twenty-year-old Cumbrian cobbler might find it tricky getting it together.

The matching software identifies people with similar jobs, political outlooks and interests. Many sites have detailed questionnaires which are as clever as a computer cupid can be – one site we list uses a sexy version of psychometric profiling. The more detail you give about yourself, the more precise the matching will be.

Online dating is good news for women. There are more males on dating sites than females, on average about 60 per cent male to 40 per cent female members. This is the opposite of traditional dating agencies, which struggle to find good – excuse the *Carry On* entendre – male members. Women who are thinking of spending hundreds of pounds for a traditional dating agency should consider trying the internet first. They will save money, and be chased rather than the chaser.

Some sites are more female-friendly than others. If you're apprehensive about dating, start with a site that has no instant messaging facility. That way, you won't feel overwhelmed by people demanding live chat every time you log on.

As well as looking for a site with a lot of frogs to turn into princes/princesses, find a place where 'your kind of people' hang out. Some sites are aimed at younger people, some at professional urbanites, others target 30-somethings ready to nest, educated types, or suburban life. We give the flavour of the sites – including the most popular – in our site reviews below.

Caveat dater

Several websites refused to tell us how many members they have – deeming the information 'confidential' – in other words, they don't want us to know. Others count membership as everyone who has created a profile since the launch, cunningly including people who never paid for membership and – unless the site is free – have never been contactable. These figures include thousands who are no longer active, so a site whose 'membership' is presented like this is creating the illusion of more activity than is really present.

But what good is a member if he or she hasn't used the service in over three months? What you need to know is the 'active' membership. Where possible, we have given this – typically the number of people who have logged on in the past three months.

Check out a site before parting with any money. Many daters tell stories of signing up to sites which boast 'membership' in the hundreds of thousands, only to find that there was little activity to support such claims.

Top UK sites according to visits		
Rank	Site	Market share (%)
1	www.gaydar.co.uk	15.01
2	www.udate.com	8.60
3	uk.personals.yahoo.com	7.84
4	www.loopylove.com	5.46
5	www.datingdirect.com	5.32
6	www.friendsreuniteddating.co.uk	3.82
7	www.match.com	3.49
8	www.friendfinderinc.com	2.51
9	love.lycos.co.uk	2.48
10	www.meetic.co.uk	2.11

Source: Hitwise, www.hitwise.co.uk (February 2005)

Site reviews

www.datetheuk.com

They say: 'Date the UK is aimed at young daters. The average age is 25 and the themes are fun and flirting. We have online chat, postcode-based location search and an integrated textflirting service so that you can register your mobile phone and send SMS messages to other members for around 20p a message without giving out your mobile number. Women on Date the UK flirtback free if a man starts to chat to them. We've also got a virtual boyfriend, who runs promotions and competitions for us.'

We say: Friendly site, which attracts the type of crowd you'd find holidaying in the Costas. There are interesting membership perks, including free happy hours, live online chat, text flirting, and a 'soulmate' lifetime membership for £69.99. (Though a lifetime membership to a dating site might be a slightly disheartening purchase.) They offer a free 48-hour trial for people who complete profile and picture.

Usability: Easy to join with a quick and simple profile system

Cost: £14.99 for one month

Membership: 230,000

M to F: 70:30

www.datingagency.com

They say: Launched in May 2001 as a mass-market online dating site for those looking for a lifetime partner. 'With an average age of 35 for women and 37 for men, we are the Marks and Spencer's of internet dating.'

We say: This site clearly veers towards a middle-aged market which is serious about finding a partner. Free of many of the more low-brow 'gimmicks' of youthier sites, it even has a 'love guarantee': equivalent to a life-time membership – or the time it takes you to find love and log off. Profiles allow for quite a bit of free expression so you get a good idea of what people are about. An unusual touch is the opportunity to 'earmark' people as intelligent, funny or attractive. This information is passed on to the particular member and used to make lists of the most popular members. Nice that these are based on other members' votes and not decided by the site, as often this becomes an opportunity to showcase the most attractive members. Another unique feature is the Russell Grant astrological matching mechanism. It's also free to send kisses and winks and find out who your fans are.

Usability: User-friendly with a human touch

Cost: £20 for one month. Twelve months plus the Love Guarantee costs £70.

Membership: 370,000

M to F: 60:40

www.datingdirect.com

They say: Dating Direct claims to be 'the UK's largest dating service with over 2 million members'. Part of a huge operation, it bills itself as a straightforward, no-frills dating service free from 'gimmicks like nicknames, free trials, and un-moderated chat rooms'.

We say: As you might expect from the mother of UK dating sites, the type of punter pitching for trade here is varied and hard to pin down. You are just as likely to meet a builder with zero qualifications as a managing director with half an alphabet after his or her name. For a service this size, it exhibits a fair lack of 'sleaze'. This is due in part to a no nicknames policy – a bonus for women who don't want to wade through 'junk mail' from count-less Bigboys and TripleXXXs. The graphics are clean and modern, and you can do a postcode search. Some users report that the number of active profiles doesn't seem to match DD's boast to be the biggest in the country.

Usability: A tidy and easy-to-use site. Well set up for international dating: click on the US, New Zealand or Australian flags if you're looking for partners there. You can have a three-day trial for £4.95.

Cost: £19.95 for one month

Membership: 1.5 million

M to F: Confidential

www.friendsreuniteddating.co.uk

They say: 'In 2003 we launched Friends Reunited Dating and transferred all the Online Personals members over to the new service. Every day we have over 1,000 new members join the service, aged from 18 to 100 and from all over the country. A dating site for genuine people of all ages who want a simple hassle-free experience for half the price of most other dating sites.' Sister sites in Australia (www.friendsreuniteddating.com.au) and New Zealand (www.findakiwidate.co.nz).

We say: The dating arm of the hugely successful Friends Reunited brand feels rather conservative: you almost expect to see photos of men washing their car. People are introduced with an amalgamation of their personal details which can read like an intro on *Blind Date*:'Hi my name is HappyNorfolkMan. I am a 31-year-old single man with light brown hair and brown eyes living in Southampton.' But persevere, because this is a friendly and easygoing place to date, with clean and well-laid-out graphics.

Usability: Basic search facilities. There's a good geographical spread and male to female ratio. If you want value for money and a site free from metropolitan snobs, this might be for you.

Cost: £9.50 for one month

Active membership: UK: 300,000, Australia: 24,269, New Zealand: 1,411

M to F: 50:50

www.guardiansoulmates.com

They say: The newspaper put its Soulmates personals online in 2004. The site is separate from its classified ads, but 'is a true extension of the newspaper … matching people with common attitudes, values and interests'. The site gets 2,000 new members every month.

We say: There's little surprise that the *Guardian* took its famous brand of love matching online. The site is well-organised, with good search and matching facilities. Members reflect the paper's liberal, worldly values. The site is a natural home for singleton artists, writers and media types who can check their mail on breaks from writing their novel or hanging their latest exhibition. Notions of PC *Guardian* males being too enlightened for totty chasing are shattered by the list of popular Soulmates women – an attractive picture and an alluring profile and you're straight into the top twenty.

Usability: A clean and easy-to-use interface. An optional voice message facility lets you hear the charming tones of potential matches. The only site with more women than men.

Cost: £16.95 for one month

Active membership: 14,000

M to F: 48:52

www.ivorytowers.net

They say: 'Ivory Towers is a matchmaking and friendship service for graduates who want to meet like-minded people with similar experiences. A shared approach to life can hold the key to establishing successful and lasting relationships.'

We say: Joining is reminiscent of filling in a college application. This site makes no bones about being an exclusive club for university graduates, threatening to check the degree certificates of unqualified pretenders. Members' photos look a bit like a librarians' convention, but the discussion boards are lively, reflecting a creative, intelligent and sparky bunch who – despite their Mallory Towers dress sense – wouldn't bore you to death on a date.

Usability: Tidy and well-designed graphics and a friendly chat forum make what could seem like a rather stern site a nice place to visit. The ten-day trial membership is a fully working one but limits you to sending five messages within a 24-hour period.

Cost: £12.95 for one month

Membership: Confidential

M to F: Confidential

www.loveandfriends.com

They say: Based in London, this is a British site – though they 'are open to members from anywhere except outer space'. Members tend to be single professionals but, as its name suggests, it is also a place to meet new 'activity partners' and 'like-minded people for some stimulating conversation'.

We say: L&F is where the frappuccino generation search for someone to peer at over their morning croissant. The site is a favourite with academics, journalists and media folk – usernames like Alphafelix or Athenaeum reflect a membership who stayed awake in Latin class. It's nice that it actively advocates friendship, which can take the edge off the mechanical feel of online dating. A lively forum section, a book club and regular meets help bolster the 'friends' element.

Usability: Easy to navigate. Profiles encourage free expression – handy if you're a dab hand at writing a self sales 'pitch'. L&F also offers a free 'ID check': members can visit the London office and have their identity verified and a 'stamp' placed on their profile confirming that they are definitely the person they say they are. L&F says this doubles the responses from women to men.

Cost: Free (three emails every 24 hours). Full membership (£10) adds unlimited use.

Membership: 50,000

M to F: 50:50

www.lovefinder.co.uk

They say: Joined the action in June 2000, 'aimed at singles of all ages, with an average of thirty to forty-somethings'. They offer an anonymous search so that you won't be listed when viewing other members. Their unique selling point is a personality-based matching engine, which differs from virtually every other dating site because 'we use a custom built Artificial Intelligence system for matching personality types. We believe simply searching for blue eyed, brown haired people aged 35 is not the way to find life partners, instead finding someone who you are compatible with personality wise is more important first, if they happen to have blue eyes and brown hair that is a bonus!'

We say: This is a no-frills site, with no space in the profile for members to describe themselves. A search for matches results in fewer hits than you would expect from a site which claims 70,000 members. The graphics look like they were lifted from an 80s video game. You don't get a lot of pleasure for your pound here, but it is a bit cheaper than the all-singing and all-dancing sites.

Usability: Simple to join and easy to navigate

Cost: £9.99 for one month

Membership: 70,000

M to F: 65:35

www.match.com

They say: 'We welcome all single adults seeking one-to-one relationships ranging from companionship to friendship, romance to marriage. Our sole purpose is to provide a fun, secure online environment with fast, relevant and lasting results. On 30 March 1996 the first baby of a Match.com-inspired marriage was born, and to date we have confirmed at least 50 more babies, more than 1,300 marriages, and hundreds of thousands of relationships.'

We say: A veteran of the dating world, Match began business in 1995. Despite being part of a huge, global enterprise, the British arm of this site feels like a viable online community. This is, in part, due to the site's very positive 'everybody's at it' approach and the introduction of its own online magazine, *Happen*, which takes 'a frank, funny look at dating and relationships' with features on such topics as 'dating tips from reality TV' and '10 couples that make us go "huh?"'. If you fancy the idea of casting your dating net over five continents, this is the site for you. Also available are gay.match.com, lesbian.match.com and senior.match.com.

Usability: A very slick site with lots of useful advice and help. There are many special features, including voice mail and matches by mobile. The online chat software feels a bit unreliable. Geographical searches can be performed down to 1 mile. A three-day free trial is available.

Cost: £17 for one month

Membership: UK: 1.2 million, Worldwide: 6 million

M to F: 60:40

www.meetic.co.uk

They say: Meetic is the most visited dating site in Europe. Its tagline is 'all you need is love'.

We say: Love is not all you need. You may also need a dictionary and lots of patience. As the name suggests, this is a European site and it shows: there are some truly unfortunate turns of phrase. In Meetic-speak, a match is a 'meetshake', and the members' gallery a 'photo zap'.

Language aside, the site works in the same way as many others. Special features include personal 'voice ads' (recorded personal greetings) and pop-up messages telling you when someone is viewing your profile and giving you the chance to respond ('You lookin' at me?' being an obvious contender).

Perhaps the last word should be left with Meetic on how to write a 'personal ad'. 'Present yourself under your best side and don't forget your sense of humour!'

Usability: Very confusing, not helped by regular, in-your-face pop-ups. These, however, allow the site to maintain a free membership. Joining and contacting other members is free of charge — great if you are immune to advertising. A Meetic pass allows you to surf the site ad-free and make more elaborate matches.

Cost: £9.50 for one month

Membership: Worldwide: 11 million

M to F: Confidential

www.midsummerseve.com

They say: One of the longest-running genuinely free sites for dating and relationships in the UK and Ireland. Midsummer's offers recordable voice profiles and online horoscopes written by starsman Russell Grant.

We say: This friendly and free site has been quietly doing its business since 1999. The graphics are simple and user-friendly. Midsummer's members are a wholesome, middle-of-the-road, straightforward bunch, with none of the airs and graces of the more 'sophisticated' sites. An antidote to the London-centric dating world, it's also a good place for single parents to partner up.

Usability: Limited search facilities, but simple to navigate

Cost: Free

Membership: 70,000

M to F: Confidential

www.myukdate.com

They say: Sister site to Date the UK, launched in April 2004. Aimed at slightly older singles looking for a relationship in the UK, with an average age of 34. It offers online chat, postcode searching, a happy hour between 5 and 7 every day when everyone can chat and mail free of charge if they have posted their picture, a free flirtback for both men and women who have posted their picture, and a message board where members can post events, jokes, etc.

We say: When Date the UK folk get a mortgage and switch from Radio 1 to 2 they move over here. Friendly and well run, with a real UK identity, the message boards give this site a homely and happy feel. The real-time chat works just like Windows messenger, and shows the picture and profile of the person you are chatting with.

Usability: Easy to set up a profile, simple to navigate and use

Cost: £14.99 for 60 days

Membership: 26,000

M to F: 70:30

www.okcupid.com

They say: A 'totally free matching service', which uses personality tests to calculate members' 'match percentage' against other members.

We say: A popular 'youth' orientated site. If the abundance of Americanisms doesn't put you off, you can easily lose yourself in the tests – the more you answer, the more you are 'understood'. A sense of humour (or is that humor?) is essential, as is the need not to be easily shocked (for example by the how-good-are-you-at-head test).

Usability: Easy to navigate – even for the most technophobic technophobe

Cost: Free

Membership: 325,000

M to F: 50:50

personals.nerve.com

They say: 'Personals for people who don't need personals.' Unlike most dating sites, the personals on Nerve are just one aspect of the *Salon*, *Onion* and *Nerve* online magazines. As a consequence they reflect the readership of the netzines, most of whom wouldn't use dedicated dating sites. Payment is by a system of credits, encouraging people to be more selective about who they contact.

We say: Nerve are trying to redefine online flirting, with their tongue-in-cheek, urban and urbane vibe. Full of esoteric monikas and coded tag lines, this Manhattan-esque dating site is so cool it could end global warming. The credit payment system is an interesting variation and may be a solution to the scattergun dating spam which infects many dating sites. But if you use a lot of credits, you may well end up spending more than a monthly fee elsewhere.

Usability: Ultra-slick, good-looking site. In terms of dating trickery, ahead of the rest – even allows you to create multiple profiles

Cost: $25 for 25 credits

Membership: UK: 12,000

M to F: 65:35

personals.yahoo.com

They say: America's biggest online dating site, a top-three UK site and a favourite in Australia and New Zealand. 'We have an easy-to-use and effective search facility. Aimed at a mainstream single market between 25 and 45 from all walks of life – from professionals to single parents, the gay community to seniors.'

We say: Once you get past the worry of the word Yahoo appearing in the same sentence as internet dating, you will find a broad crowd, on a busy, efficient site which should satisfy most daters.

Usability: An easy-to-use interface which lets you find local matches with a postcode search. It also has a 'find similar match' facility, which tries to locate similar types to people you like.

Cost: £16.95 for one month

Active membership: UK: 150,000, Worldwide: 5 million

M to F: 60:40

www.snoglondon.com

They say: 'Where the capital comes to kiss.' The site was set up in January 2003. Members are mainly heterosexual singles aged between 21 and 40. A very laid-back site, it celebrates the fact that online dating is 'coming out', and is no longer taboo.

We say: This (shocking pink) site has a cheeky take on internet romance. The dating-lite approach means it attracts as many Londoners looking to make friends as find lovers. The 'favourite quotes' question on members' profiles (with answers such as 'What will be will be') reveals a site that doesn't attract the more academic singleton, but instead takes a very light-hearted view of online dating. The younger generation are well catered for, so if your target date is a 'Juicy Jacky' rather than a 'Jacqueline1962', this is the place to be. However, if you're looking for in-depth conversations about world events steer well clear.

Usability: Pretty straightforward. The site is notable for its excellent 'customer service' and useful dating tips. Some cute touches: you can send people virtual kisses or a virtual snowstorm.

Cost: £5 for one month or £50 for a year

Active membership: 5,000

M to F: 65:35

www.udate.com

They say: Originating in the US, the site is aimed at 'fun, dating and long term relationships'. They boast 5,000 new members a day – making it the 'fastest-growing romance, matchmaking and dating site on the net'. Udate claim to have the very latest and most comprehensive matchmaking facilities, enabling members to quickly identify and communicate with people who meet their exact criteria.

We say: Udate is a large worldwide site – something of an über-site. You can see if a member is online, and its 'whisper' feature allows for – rather slow – live chat. The 'encounters' section brings out the cyber spy in you, as it shows who has viewed your profile and when. Add to this the members' gallery – and the fact that it can feel a bit like a jungle for women who get hit on by all species of cyberdating life – and you can see why the site has earned the nickname 'Zoodate'. The upside of this is that you can get to know people quickly. There is a good geographical spread of members from all walks of life: from single parents to 30-something professionals. If you avoid the 'meat-head' quota among male members (with inspiring user names such as Luca the Fuca, Clittickler and Foryourpleasure), with a bit of patience you can find some interesting folk. A good point is that you can tell if a member is paying (Gold) and can return your messages.

Usability: The profile section doesn't offer a lot of room for self-description, and some of the standard questions tend to put people in boxes. Good if you are short on time, and don't like talking about yourself.

Cost: £19.99 for one month

Membership: Confidential

M to F: Confidential

www.wheresmydate.co.uk

They say: 'An exciting and personality-driven UK dating service made up of a fun, high-quality group of singles from all walks of life, professions and ages. Wheresmydate.com is designed to bring people together in a safe, relaxed atmosphere.'

We say: A run-of-the-mill site with knobs on. The overall impression is a site which has been put together in a hurry. It tries hard to distinguish itself from other sites by asking members a series of questions called 'can-openers' (let's hope there are no worms inside). The problem is that none of this shows up in search results where all you get is a very basic physical description and photo accompanied by the member's star sign. For the moment this feels like a sparsely populated site, but irritations aside, this is an inoffensive, friendly site tailor-made for UK singles.

Usability: Helps if you're a fan of bright lollipop colours and astrology

Cost: £14.95 for one month

Membership: Confidential

M to F: 60:40

Chapter 3

THE LANGUAGE OF LOVE

How to Write a Good Profile

In internet dating the profile is everything. How you pitch yourself and what you choose to include could be the difference between dating success and dating disaster. The good news is that the more online dating you do, the more adept at it you become.

Even when you've posted a photograph, cyberdating revolves around the written word – and what those words conjure up in the mind of the person reading them. One awkward turn of phrase and you could send whole swathes of potential matches reaching for their mouse.

Internet dating turns us all into amateur psychologists – each trying to penetrate the personality behind the profile. It's not what you write that counts, but what the reader thinks:

She writes: Voluptuous 30-something female, surprised to find herself single, enjoys nights in and quality time with family.

He thinks: Overweight woman, about to hit 40, hasn't dated for years and still lives at home with her parents.

He writes: Tactile, sensual guy who's open to new experiences.

She thinks: Perv.

You quickly learn to read between the lines, developing a 'weeding' process to decide what is and what isn't 'acceptable'. Often that decision is made in the space of a few seconds. Some daters take a scattergun approach – a glance at the photo, a cursory read of a profile and they're away: firing off email after random email. Others employ a strict vetting procedure – which varies according to gender.

What women see in men's profiles

For women it's important to keep an eye out for 'nutters' – the internet 'bogeymen' that stop many women going online in the first place.

It's worth remembering, though, that meeting a man in cyberspace is no more dangerous than being chatted up in a bar or nightclub (see Safety box on page ix). The only difference is that without the sensual aid of a face-to-face encounter – gesture, tone of voice, etc. – women learn to rely on a different set of signals.

One woman from Dating Direct says: 'I always read a profile twice. Once for warning signs, and once for sense.' And the warning signs? 'I always have one eye open for signs of depression, anger, and perviness of course.'

Another dater from Match says: 'If a profile is only two lines long, I wonder what he's got to hide. A full profile with lots of detail means he's more likely to be open in real life.'

What men see in women's profiles

Men have different 'dangers' in mind. 'I look for signs of bunny-boilers in the photograph and in the profile', says a dater from Love and Friends. 'Repetition, denial, too much emphasis on being normal … too much self-deprecation. Even too many comments in brackets which are the online equivalent of "Sorry!" Another says: 'I avoid women who are sexually explicit – they're either nymphomaniacs or trying to be something they're not. Either way it's not a good sign.'

Of course this detective work is not necessarily conscious and it's not always that rigorous. But it gives you an idea of the filtering process most of us employ, consciously or otherwise.

How to give good profile

In dating terms, a profile is the online personality you create for yourself. How detailed this is largely depends on the site. Some sites merely require you to tick boxes and answer multiple choice questions about your interests and physical appearance; others provide so much space for you to describe yourself, you need a day off work.

Multiple choice

Try to complete as many sections as possible. If you leave large chunks blank, it may give the impression that either you're hiding something or you just couldn't be bothered. In any case, it will limit the number of responses you get.

Tick-boxes have a tendency to steer profiles in directions they might not normally have travelled. Many people wouldn't dream of lying in the 'In your own words' section – but given multiple choice it can be tempting to be creative with the truth. As Martin from Udate says, 'The problem with profiles by numbers is that they tempt people to present an idea of who they want to be rather than who they really are. If you buy the *Sun*, don't claim to be a *Guardian* reader.'

Some people clearly tick the boxes they think will net them more responses. Nowhere is this more prevalent – and more ill-advised – than in the 'physical appearance' section.

What women lie about

Age: Every dating site has them – Whitneys posing as Britneys. The question is why? Do women think men are that stupid?

A Dating Direct member says: 'I contacted a woman who started off as 19 and unmarried from Manchester. During the course of our correspondence, she gradually revealed she was 42, married with kids and living in Tunbridge Wells.'

Another, very cynical, dater says: 'Never trust a woman who claims to be 39!' Why? 'Because it usually translates as 40 and beyond!'

Physique: The multiple choices are a minefield of euphemisms: average, shapely, voluptuous, slightly overweight or large, forcing you into the position of second-guessing your reader. If you really are voluptuous and tick that, many men will steer clear anyway, because their internal translator reads 'fat'. Our advice is to be as honest as possible and you'll lessen the likelihood of embarrassment later on. And don't forget many men like women with curves.

What men lie about

Height: Don't lie about your height – there's nothing worse on a date than expecting Daniel Day-Lewis and having Danny DeVito show up.

Hair: Don't put 'salt and pepper' if the pepper mill has been empty for years. There's no point putting wavy/straight if that applies to the one remaining hair on your head. And anyway, many women find bald men very attractive.

Conversely some daters play *down* their assets, in case they count against them. 'I've met women who'll tick the degree box in the Education section because they think that a Masters would be too intimidating!' says a Jdate member. Jane, a GP on Dating Direct, dumbs down too. 'I just say I'm "in medicine" because most men put doctors in the same bracket as their mother.'

One woman from Udate had a disastrous evening because her date ticked the 'social drinker' box – yet in reality didn't drink at all. 'He lied because he didn't want people to think he was "uptight". Consequently, as I got more drunk and more animated, he just became more subdued and embarrassed.'

What's in a name?

Choosing a screen-name may seem an innocuous task. However, what you call yourself may determine the number of responses you get, so it's worth giving it some thought. Some people won't look at your profile if they don't like your name. And you'd be amazed at how offensive a name can be.

Naff name types – women

- Page 3: 'Foxychick', 'SeXXXy', 'LittleMinx', 'Quim'. It might be a joke to you but imagine what it says to them! 'Often, these are the same women who complain that they're not taken seriously!' says Ben from Jdate.
- Twee: 'Teletubby', 'Tinkerbell', 'Pussycat'. As Pete from Love and Friends puts it, 'These'll be the ones with a cuddly toy collection and an "Ah! Bless!" habit.'
- High maintenance: 'Luxurychick', 'Littleprincess', 'Amworthit'. They don't need a boyfriend; they need an expense account.

Naff name types – men

- Lord of the Rings: 'Darkrider', 'Trackfrower', 'Fierceheart'. How many women want a man whose idea of a good night out is dressing up in Goth-gear and battling the forces of darkness?
- Cheesy: 'MAN4YOU', '2good2betrue', 'JovialJon', 'Topgeeza'. Fine – if you fancy a date with Chaz 'n' Dave.
- Hardcore: 'Spunkmeister', 'Love69', 'Cumwithme'. Need we say more?

So how do you pick an appealing screen-name? A good idea is to see this as your chance to have the name you've always wanted. This could be as simple as using your favourite name or borrowing the name of a fictional favourite. But bear in mind that while 'Travis' or 'Bickle' may not ring alarm bells for many daters, 'Hannibal' or 'Lecter' probably will. Another idea is to refer to something in your profile, for example an interest (Masterchef, La Boheme, MarathonMan), your favourite band or song (Moloko, Uptown Girl, FranklyMrShankly) – or even where you live, within reason: 'Slough chick' doesn't have quite the same ring to it as 'Islington babe'.

The pitch

After the photo, the 'in your own words' section is the most scrutinised part of a profile. Many people skip the multiple-choice starter and go straight to the main course. We can't provide you with a profile-on-a-plate, but we can pinpoint some of the mistakes people make and give you some suggestions for how to get it right.

To look at the majority of profiles on the net, anybody would think we were a nation of sheep — all trying to compete for the title of Mr and Ms Dating Average:

> **Genuine guy**. Intelligent, sensitive, easy-going, attractive with a great personality and a gsoh. Loves going out and staying in. Enjoys all the usual pursuits – restaurants, films, theatre, art galleries. Looking for someone of a similar age, and with similar interests.

What's wrong with it? What's right with it? On some sites, there are up to half a million profiles. To increase your chances of success, make your profile stand out, not merge in with the rest.

This 'catch-all' profile, the most common type, relies on long lists of adjectives, which become meaningless after a while. Rather than *saying* you're funny, *be* funny. Instead of claiming intelligence, *be* intelligent. Anybody who has to say they have 'a great personality' probably doesn't.

Instead of listing 'art galleries', name those you prefer, whether it's the Tate Modern or the tiniest, most obscure gallery in Wapping. As for films, there's a whole world of difference between Jean-Claude Van Damme and Jean de Florette.

One way of tackling this is to take a 'these are a few of my favourite things' approach:

> **Manchester-based architect** likes: Ken Loach, Harold Pinter, vanilla, poppies, being by water, St John's in Didsbury, Stella Artois, Andy Warhol, The Lowry Museum, Ricky Gervais. Dislikes: celery, spitting, Shania Twain, Mike Myers, parsnips, noisy/bright pubs, trolleys left in car park spaces, putting duvet covers on.

However, be careful not to go too far down the Julie Andrews 'whiskers-on-kittens' route. And don't come over all high-brow if it's not really you. It could come back to haunt you:

❝I pretended I liked opera, and then had to sit through four and a half hours of Wagner on our first date because he'd bought front row seats. **❞**

Karen, Dating Direct

Think of your profile as the start of a conversation and give the other party something to latch on to. That way, you're more likely to receive better replies – 'Yeah, I like Ricky Gervais/that gastropub in Didsbury too', instead of the standard 'I liked your profile', which reads as 'I didn't actually read your profile, but I liked your picture.'

Be aware of what you're writing and how it could be interpreted – or *mis*interpreted. Read it a couple of times and ask yourself 'Would I want to meet me?' Strike a good balance: you don't want to show off but equally you don't want to come across as so self-deprecating, you need help.

Look at other profiles, find one that appeals and try to work out why. But resist the temptation to copy it word for word and add another profile clone to the mix.

Lastly, remember to do a spell-check – if a profile is badly written or teeming with typos, what does it say about you?

Bad profiles

In Britain, selling yourself, aka blowing your own trumpet, is considered very poor taste. It's no coincidence that numerous profiles start with the words 'I hate talking about myself' or 'Where to begin?' Others take the cop-out 'My friends would describe me as …' route.

This may explain why so many daters fill their profiles with corny one-liners culled from tacky TV shows and the kind of cheesy phrases that Mills and Boon would be proud of. When these are set alongside a thousand other clichés on a dating site, they seem so well-worn as to be laughable.

The top ten dating clichés:

1. Enjoy all the usual pursuits (Come on, love, try a bit harder.)
2. Zany/wacky/crazy kind of guy/girl (Anybody who claims to be wacky is guaranteed to be dull.)
3. Enjoy nights in and nights out (And the alternative would be?)
4. Genuine guy (If he has to say he's genuine, chances are he's not.)
5. Surprisingly single (And the rest of us take it for granted?)
6. Romantic-walk-in-the-country-followed-by-candlelit-dinner-by-log-fire-in-country-pub as their 'ideal date' (Barbara Cartland is dead.)
7. I'm a mass of contradictions (And the rest of us are all one-dimensional?)
8. I love to laugh (Does anybody hate it?)
9. I'm looking for that 'special someone' (While we're looking for Mr/Ms Ordinary.)
10. I can't believe I'm doing this (Thereby insulting everybody else on the site.)

It's easy to turn people off. For example:

Women:
- 'who say "I'm kind, caring, compassionate" and go on to write: "Creeps, boring gits or people under 5'5" need not apply" – far too judgmental!' (Sam, Dating Direct)
- 'who slag off their exes – they're obviously bitter and twisted' (David, Jdate)
- 'who put "No time for game-playing" – guaranteed if you contact them, they'll start playing games' (Mitchell, Makefriendsonline)

Men:

- 'who say "I live life to the max" – but spend their whole time in chat rooms!' (Sara, Match)
- 'who write "I've done this, I've done that in my bachelor days, but now I'm ready for commitment" – I mean, "Congrat-u-bleedin-lations!"' (Susan, Makefriendsonline)
- 'who promise to treat you like a "real lady" – reminds me of the *Fast Show*'s Swiss Toni (fine wines and Belgian chocolates) character' (Caroline, Wheresmydate)

Sometimes it's not just the odd line that makes you cringe – it's the whole profile.

The 'show-off':

> **Limited offer!** I've just been head-hunted by a leading law firm so I'm returning to the UK after 7 years in L.A & NYC. I'm keen to pursue my doctorate (I have 3 degrees) and start a family. A domestic god and an ace cook, I'm well travelled (lived in all 5 continents), well-read, and well-preserved. Both drop-dead gorgeous and dazzlingly brilliant, I'm also great with kids (must be the mud pies and ghost stories). I like to work hard and play hard – I beat my personal record in the NY marathon this year, did it in 3 h 45. I own houses in London (Butlers Wharf), NY and Paris; a beautiful racehorse (the beautiful Bella); oh, and a yacht in Bermuda where I plan to spend the summer. Maybe you'll join me.

This man has mistaken his profile for a job application. You can see him now: he'll have a perma-tan and one of those motorbikes the size of a small house, call women 'girlies', listen to Billy Joel and have a name for his penis. Many women would feel at best mildly amused and at worst incredibly intimidated.

The 'comedian':

> **If I can't make you laugh, I'll give you your money back!**
> Hello! Thanks for stopping by! Oh you pressed the wrong button? Too bad!*@. I'm 42 but could easily pass for 40. Mature? I tried it once and it didn't fit! Yes, I'm a little bit overweight, (LOL) but as long as you've got bigger bosoms than me, that's great! In the looks department, I'm 5'10" and cuddly. You could take me home to your mother. I won't dribble, honest. Hobbies include am dram, (more am than dram ☺) cinema, eating out and eating in. I'm looking for someone smart, funny and curvy. It's like I always say: If you're gonna get one, get a big one! xxxx

You can see him now: the office 'clown' in a novelty tie, a jumper his mum knitted him for Christmas, and over-sized blue glasses circa 1979. Just stick to humour that makes you human and friendly, not frightening.

The 'princess':

> I'm a super bright, utterly gorgeous girl, who always gets what she wants – so if you can't stand the pace, I suggest you leave the kitchen. I want a lover, not a loser, so if you're insecure, over-sensitive, or earn under £100K, forget it! A perfect evening would start with cocktails at Bambu, move on to dinner at Sketch, and wind down with drinks at Hakasaan. A perfect weekend? Shopping in New York or sailing in the Seychelles. I deserve a man who is thoughtful and clever, who prefers his club to a pub, who rows, plays tennis and can keep me in the manner to which I am accustomed. If you're under 6 ft, indecisive, unfit or ugly don't email me – it really, really isn't worth it.

You will never measure up to Ms Spoiled-brat's standards. Only a masochist would reply.

The 'flake':

> Hi there! I'm an elegant, intelligent, young 40-some-thing who's looking for the missing piece in the jigsaw. I've had my share of ups and downs :- (and I recognise that I have some catching up to do. Life is a journey – the path is wide but the way is never clear. I have recently enrolled on a 'Happiness Now – Life as a Celebration' course. I enjoy African drumming, callig-raphy, papermaking and meditation – I just completed a breathing weekend in Bath, which released a new bud in me. I'm seeking a man who has explored himself. Someone whose heart beats in rhythm with mine.

As John from Jdate put it, 'It makes you want to write an email saying:"Sorry but I can't afford the psychiatric help you so clearly need."'

Good profiles

Okay, so not many profiles are *that* bad, but many could be improved.

One of the advantages of online dating is that profiles are not set in stone. Nor does it cost any money to update them. So if your profile doesn't elicit the response you want the first time round, go back and change it.

Bear in mind that the more honest a picture you paint of yourself, the better your chances will be. Judging from our experience, and that of the internet daters we talked to (see box), the appeal of a profile can usually be narrowed down to a few essential ingredients:

- Humour
- Honesty
- Hooks, for example likes/dislikes
- Good grammar/punctuation/style
- Originality
- A lightness of touch (i.e. not overtly sexual or over the top)
- Warmth
- Modesty

Use these and you'll stand every chance of success.

Profile appeal

❝I like honesty and logic – women who resonate as grounded, don't show off and don't mind downplaying themselves. Who tell it like it is, i.e. who say they would prefer to be in a relationship rather than single. **❞**

Tony, Dating Direct

❝The ones that admit that occasionally they like sitting around doing absolutely nothing – at least it's honest. Most people sound like they're into everything under the sun – you just think, do they ever stop? **❞**

Karen, Wheresmydate

❝I like anything that's genuinely amusing, especially irony. I also like women who can be self-deprecating and who include some negative attributes – it makes them seem more genuine. **❞**

Richard, Jdate

❝I prefer it if they're honest about why they're doing it rather than pretending it's just something they happened to do in an idle moment. **❞**

Fiona, Udate

Chapter 4

A SHOT IN THE DARK

Choosing a Good Photograph

We can almost guarantee that once you start dating online, you'll never look at a Lonely Hearts column again. The old-fashioned method of blind dating now seems so, well, blind. You speak for hours on the phone, you get steamed up with anticipation, and then – BOOM! – you meet and it's all over before you can say, 'You'll never believe it, but my sister's just gone into labour and I have to go to the hospital.'

The beauty of online dating is its ability to provide you with at least an *idea* of what a person looks like from the start. We're not saying that looks are everything – far from it – but for most daters, physical attraction is vital. When people have a choice of profiles with or without photos, nine times out of ten, they'll choose the visuals.

But the idea of posting a photograph on the net stops some daters dead in their tracks. Often it's the one reason why they refuse to go online at all. The explanations are varied – they're 'scared of being spotted by people they know', it's humiliating 'advertising oneself like a piece of meat', or they're worried they're not attractive enough.

On the other hand, there are some – often very attractive women – who prefer not to post their photos on the net for fear of getting too much attention. They opt to email their photos once they've built up a relationship. Some sites accommodate this by giving you the option of posting photos 'only for my friends' – so that only the members you've earmarked as favourites/buddies/friends will be able to view your picture.

Whatever your reason, consider the message that not posting a photo gives out. Okay, some might assume you're too ugly, or too shy, but the overriding message is: you're not bothered about finding a date. This impression is often reinforced by a lack of detail in the rest of the profile – profiles without photos are usually the most sketchy.

Show me yours, I'll show you mine

A lack of a photograph makes people think you're not 'playing the game'. It's a question of solidarity: online dating is a great leveller – with everybody in the same boat. You wouldn't go out with your mates and leave your wallet behind – so if you're serious about looking for love, post a photo – it shows willing and makes potential matches feel that they are on an equal footing.

There is another, very important, reason why most daters prefer profiles with photos. A no-show on men's profiles, in particular, can make women – who assess men's personalities by looking at them – very uneasy.

A blatant refusal to post a picture makes me think there's something fishy going on – which is always a worry because you never know who is hiding behind any profile in reality.

Sarah, Udate

I wouldn't dream of talking to someone without a photo. Why would I want to? That's too creepy for words.

Karen, Jdate

❝Any photo is better than no photo. In this day and age of digital cameras and mobile phones, there is no excuse for not having a picture up.❞

Sue, Snog London

Many of those who do post photos won't consider replying to people who don't (unless the rest of their profile is fantastically convincing). The overall feeling is: 'You've seen mine, now show me yours!' Most websites offer searches for 'profiles with photo only', so chances are that without a picture, many potential matches simply won't see your profile at all.

The most compelling argument for including a photo, however, is this: profiles with photographs attract ten times more responses than those without. A survey by Match showed men are 14 times more likely to look at a profile with a photo and women 8.5 times more likely.

That said, the photos that some daters choose are so unappealing, they would probably fare better without!

Photo no-nos

You would think that it's obvious how to present yourself on a dating site. Good, clear picture, nice smile. You'd be wrong.

Many people harbour the illusion that they can use any old photo and still get dates. And some people's idea of what constitutes sex appeal is so far removed from reality, it beggars belief.

If a woman is looking for a serious relationship, why does she post a picture doing her best Melinda Messenger impersonation? Yet it happens. As Richard from Wheresmydate puts it, 'So many times I've seen the words "Dirty old men and lechers need not apply" next to a photo best described as Readers'

Wives!' The same goes for men – what does naked from the waist up say about you – other than 'vain'? Or, as is often the case, deluded?

Women – we recommend you swap the overtly sexual shot for one where you are fully clothed, smiling – and relaxed. By that we don't mean drunk. The good-time-girl look won't appeal to everyone. Choose a more neutral photo, and you'll net a wider range of guys. Let them find out the truth later.

Men – the same applies to the rugger-bugger shots with your trousers around your ankles. Okay, that's an exaggeration, but you get the idea. Photos of you having a laugh with the lads might not be a winner with the ladies.

Macho posturing

Remember the actors' maxim 'never work with children or animals' – or any other prop for that matter. Especially when it's of the 'Look what I've got – na-na!' variety. You'd be amazed how many men pose next to their car (even when it's a Ford Escort), motorbike, powerboat or, in some cases, borrowed blonde. This won't wash with many women. 'I just think SAD', says one dater. 'If a man needs to endorse himself with some status symbol, what does that say about his personality?'

'I hate the "I've got something to prove" shots', says Julie from Jdate. 'The "I'm Mr Adventurous, me, run-the-New-York-marathon-swum-with-dolphins-and-jumped-off-Everest – and-here's-me-playing-with-a-lion-cub" photograph.'

❝My worst is the power desk photograph. Where the guy has his feet up on the desk or is so important, he's on the phone. **❞**

Paula

Girlie posturing

Equally, men may not be impressed by women snuggling up to their cat, dog, or cuddly toy collection. 'They're the type who do baby-talk and expect you to say you've missed them when they've popped out for ten minutes', says Andy from Jdate.

'Cat photos are a big red flag to me. I instantly think: "oh, sad, lonely spinster surrounded by cats and yellowing newspapers, eating cold baked beans out of a can". Also if the cat's so important it's in the photo, then you suspect that unless Mr Tibbles likes you, the relationship won't go far.'

Women doing the 'man thing' and posing next to their latest acquisition may not go down well either. 'I really hate shots of women with sports cars – you don't need to be as stupid as a man to get equality!' says Gary from Udate.

The technical aspect

Make sure you can be seen in the photo. This may sound obvious (if not ridiculous) but the net is full of photos where it's so dark, you can't make out the face, so distant, the head is a mere speck, or so close, it's distorted in a *Blair Witch* kind of way. Not a good look, in any case. Also avoid group photos when it's not obvious which one's you.

Then there are sunglasses (banned on some sites) and ski goggles. Both can be annoying – either because you simply cannot see the person clearly or because of what it might 'say'.

❝I get so sick of people in skiing/snowboarding gear – I mean ... er, ok, so that looks like fun, but I can't see your face. And if you are able to make something out, it's usually a distant face with goggles!❞

Lis, Snog London

❝I hate pictures of men in sunglasses. It just makes me think they're married and trying to hide – that, or they've got terrible crow's feet! **❞**

Sarah, Jdate

❝You can tell a lot from someone's eyes so hiding them just makes you think: 'dodgy'. **❞**

Andrew, Match

Ex marks the spot

You'd also be wise to avoid photos with the ex (especially those with jagged edges where they've been ripped out (yes, really!).

Jackie from Love and Friends maintains this is the biggest mistake a man can make. 'It's so sad. All it says is she's the only girlfriend you've ever had or that you're so insecure about pulling, you need proof.'

Liz says: 'I think the worst photos – and this *really* bugs me – are the ones where you just *know* the last girlfriend was cut off. So you have some guy and half a head of blonde hair and suchlike to the edge of the picture and a mysterious arm around his neck. Those just make me think: loser.'

Don't assume women are off the hook here either. They're not. In fact, sometimes – okay, just occasionally – women will post a wedding photograph, the groom a distant memory (or on another dating site).

'There are also bridesmaid shots – they're also scary because they say "I want a husband now!"', says Phil from Dating Direct.

Most serious photo offences

Women

1. Group shot – with two or three faces without the 'dater' singled out
2. Page 3 – the naked head and shoulders shot
3. The dater's own wedding photo (seen three times)
4. Standing romantically against a landscape – so small you need a magnifying glass to make them out
5. Doctored photos with 'crazee' borders
6. The 'Look at me – I'm pissed' shot
7. Cutie shot – posing with cuddly toys or pet
8. Passport photo, especially when a date stamp is visible proving it's five years out of date

Men

1. Posing with 'prop' (half the men on Udate)
2. Pictures with the ex blatantly cut out – you can even see their arm on his shoulder ('Look, I did have a girlfriend once.')
3. The six-pack – i.e. half-naked, torso shot ('Leave something to the imagination, please.')
4. The webcam shot (where the person looks as if someone has just shoved a gun in his back)
5. Hat/sunglasses shot (something to declare?)
6. The Hugh Grant / Divine Brown mug-shot – scary
7. The distant shot – the speck's the head
8. Posing with cat/dog/small child
9. The joker – photos of George Clooney, Brad Pitt, even Einstein (Do these ever get a response?)

Living in the past

Of course the biggest – and most common – offence of all is using a photo that is so out of date, it doesn't reflect your current appearance at all.

Why people do this is curious. 'Sometimes', says one dater, 'it is merely a case of the person not realising how much they've changed. I met a man once whose hair was totally grey and yet he'd said it was "salt and pepper".'

Another, 30-something, woman says: 'Hair is probably where men of my age fall down. I've met blokes who are totally bald and say they're "receding", then there are men who just choose a photo where they're wearing a hat so you don't recognise them when they walk in.'

❝I did once meet a bloke who had sent me his pic, he claimed to be 6' 2", and in the photo he had quite a lot of hair and his mouth closed. When we met he was about 5' 7", had lost most of his hair and nearly all his teeth. When I told him I was leaving, he told me I was superficial and only interested in looks. My response was that if he could lie about something as obvious as his height, I would never be able to trust him about anything else. ❞

Sarah, Match

Whatever your reason, using a totally unrepresentative picture can only lead to awkwardness when you meet face-to-face. 'I waited next to a woman in a pub for a whole half hour once without realising she was my date', says Tim from Udate. 'The embarrassing thing was I eventually called her mobile which of course rang right next to me!' How come? The woman in question had posted a photo that was thirteen years out of date. (That said, those two are still together!)

The same goes for a photo that is so 'enhanced' it doesn't look like the everyday you – in other words the 'some studio in London does your hair and smears a bit of Vaseline on a lens shot', as one man put it.

This may mean avoiding black and white shots, which are very flattering, or, in the case of women, semi-professional shots where several hours in make-up have turned you into a Kylie clone.

Better to choose a nice but realistic photo and pull out all the stops on the night. That way, you'll give your date a pleasant surprise.

Picture perfect

So, to give yourself a fighting chance of being contacted, and to avoid being overlooked as you sit waiting patiently for your date in the pub, take note of our top photographic tips. First, choose a picture in which you are relaxed and happy – holiday photos are good. Second, make sure you are smiling – men in particular seem to think it's butch to frown. Third, use a recent picture and one which really looks like you – as opposed to the one-in-a-million 'fluke' that doesn't. Make sure your face is clearly visible and not obscured by sunglasses or a hat. And lastly, posting a couple of secondary photos is always good – just don't see it as an invitation to roll out the whole album.

Getting it up

To get your photo onto a dating website, you need a digital image. The easiest route is via a digital camera. Once you have a picture you are happy with, you can either plug the camera directly into a computer (via a USB plug) or have the picture copied on to a CD. If you are using a conventional camera, your print or negative will need to be scanned (go to a high-street print shop, and they will give you a CD of the picture to take away).

From your camera or CD, save the image as a file on your computer in a place where you'll easily be able to find it again. Before you can upload it to a dating site you may have to make some changes to the image. First, it will need to be a JPEG file. This means that the last letters of the file name must be .JPG. Second, you will have to make the file size (*not* the actual dimensions of the photo) small enough for the upload. Most sites will only accept pictures of an absolute maximum size of 30 KB. So crop and resize the picture. To do this you will need some software that manipulates pictures. If you don't have access to the likes of Photoshop you can download free basic software such as IrfanView from the internet (www.download.com/3000-2192-10021962.html).

When you go online to a dating site, you will be offered the option to browse to the file of your picture. Click on it, and upload your picture to the site. Once it is approved, your face will be online, and hopefully trigger an avalanche of mail!

Chapter 5

ANIMAL ATTRACTION

A Guide to Specialist Sites

There is no better place for birds of a feather to flock together than the internet. It brims with specialist dating sites: for the tall and the small, Christian and Muslim, pet lovers, seniors, arty types, brainiacs, the overweight, single parents, Russian brides and swingers. All are catered for so, if you have a special interest, it's a cyberspace certainty that someone is trying to pair you up with a like-minded someone else.

Supersize you?

'What build are you?' – this is the poison-chalice question posed by nearly every dating site. Some even demand the exact poundage. In a nipped-and-tucked world where excess is a negative, overweight people often find it uncomfortable – or even impossible – to date on a conventional site. So why not cut through the minefield and join a place where they celebrate the supersized?

www.bigbeautyclub.com (£30 for three months) is an international site where members are large and loud. 'Hey, I'm a big bouncy bubbly bird', alliterates Bigfatdevil from Swindon, while Bustinoutallover from Peterborough wants to big-it-up with 'people who appreciate the fuller figure'.

'Size is only a number' is the slogan of **www.largefriends. com** ($19.00 for two months). With a big selection of big UK daters, the site caters for BBW (Big Beautiful Women), BHM (Big Handsome Men), FA (Fat Admirers – men who like larger people), and FFA (Female Fat Admirers – ladies who like larger folk), so if you like your love with handles, this could be the place for you.

www.bigpeople.org.uk is a cheerful and cheap (free) UK site set up in 1977 for 'people who consider themselves big, and do not have a problem with big people'. With plenty of chat and discussions, if you want a friendly, home-made UK site this is for you.

Big time dating

'It's hard for us to date on a "normal site"', says Jo – founder of bigpeople.org. 'They don't represent Big people, the tick boxes don't even acknowledge our existence: with categories like "slim/athletic/a few extra pounds", how is a BBW or a super-BBW going to feel comfortable? We're liberated on BBW sites – you know who you'll find here, and you're not going to be rejected because of your size. It's also a place for men who have been mocked or shamed for dating big women to see that there are plenty of men who share their taste. Internet dating has changed the lives of thousands of big people who used to feel down about themselves and now feel positive.'

Love's highs

How tall are you? Another standard dating site question. The press inches dedicated to Cruise and Kidman's vertical disparity indicate that the world is yet to reach enlightenment on the height issue – men are expected to be taller than their partners.

For the very tall, particularly women, finding a partner can be tricky. **www.tallfriends.com** ($10 a month) announces itself as the place 'where tall friends and singles feel at home'. The site is US-based, but there are plenty of international members – women who are 6 foot or over and finding it hard to find a match on conventional sites might feel at home here.

Short people can find it equally hard to match up on general sites. On one hand an online search liberates a short person – letting them make contact with people whose height suits them, and telling them if their match is willing to date somebody of their height. But statistics are stacked against them. Only 10 per cent of women are willing to date men who are shorter than them and a husband is shorter than his wife in less than 1 per cent of marriages. So it's a waste of time and money for a short man to contact someone who has already made up her mind to date only tall men. A site like **www.shortpassions.com** (a free online community for short singles) is a great place for people who don't want to be judged because of their size.

The food of love

www.veggieromance.com announces itself with its logo of cherries nestling among leaves. Part of the Snog franchise, this UK-based free site for herbivore lovers has profile questions such as 'My favourite vegetarian meal' and forum debates on 'Bread – can it be trusted?' This is a snappy-looking place, which caters for both eco-warriors and well-groomed thinking urbanites.

Home alone

www.othersingleparents.com (£5 a month) calls itself 'a place to create new friendships, communicate with other single parents, to share experiences ... and find romance'. This UK site dedicated to single parents caters for a group of people who have benefited more than many others from the internet dating revolution. This is a clean and well-organised site, where nobody needs to be vague over the answer to the 'have you got children?' question.

Senior service

Perhaps the most fictionalised tick box on dating sites is age. In a world where people want to appear younger than they are, subtracting a few years on a dating site is so easy it is hard to resist. To escape from this, daters can log on to **www.seniorfriendfinder.com** ($22.95 per month), which describes itself as 'dating for people who don't see age as a barrier to love'. 'Nil desperandum', announces 56-year-old dater Perdita from Plymouth, while Serocer from Edinburgh is looking for an 'adventurous man – who is not ready to settle down yet!!!'

    www.over50sromance.com is a free UK-based 'friendship and dating site for singles over the age of fifty'. It pitches itself at 'a generation with a completely different outlook; more active, more demanding, and expecting a lot more out of life'. The atmosphere is friendly, with forum discussions on subjects such as 'too old to settle down?' and 'growing old disgracefully'.

Tales from the silver surf

One of the main obstacles to online dating for older people has been technophobia. But this is fading fast, and now over 16 per cent of people on the top five dating sites are over 55.

❝When my marriage broke down I didn't feel like going out but liked the idea of chatting and flirting through my fingers, so internet dating was the perfect solution. I was worried that my age would be a problem, but once I got into the 'swing of things' that disappeared. The general sites are starting to cater for us oldies and, in any case, I like chatting to younger men – I think they enjoy the Mrs Robinson scenario. I have single friends in a similar situation – when I talk to them I realise that our generation is still a bit wary about internet dating. But it has changed my life, and if I'm still single in ten years' time I'll still be online.**❞**

PamelaAnn, 57, My UK Date

❝I was introduced to internet dating by my daughter. A lot of us get the nudge from our offspring – several guys I have met up with have said their kids got them online. I don't find age a barrier to internet dating; obviously there are more 30-somethings on general sites than those of us in the 'senior' age range, but once I started chatting online, it felt safe and people were interesting to talk to.

I use a number of sites, including Date the UK, My UK Date, Wheresmydate, and Yahoo Personals. The first two are more user-friendly, but Yahoo has more local matches (I live in the north). There's definitely room for sites aimed at the mature age range as it would make the search easier.

> *So far there has only been one really special guy and sadly for me he didn't feel the same way. Heartbreak is just as hard at 57 as it is at 17. However, the short few weeks we spent together gave me the hope that love can still be found out there at any age and if it's happened once it can happen again – maybe next time the feelings will be mutual.*
>
> *My family are right behind me. My 80-year-old mother is fascinated by internet dating, and my young work colleagues – who were initially surprised by my dating 'antics' – have since been persuaded to join up and give it a go.* 🙸
>
> Anna, 57, Date the UK

Just one look

'You want to date the best looking person you can find. Everyone enjoys the giddy feeling of meeting someone who's smoking hot. You can get that feeling here. Come on in', boasts **www.dreammatches.com**. The only problem is that to 'come on in', your photo has to be approved by their beauty police. 'We understand this is somewhat superficial', they dissemble, 'but, lets [sic] face it. Dream Matches is a exclusive dating club for beautifil [sic] people.' Too busy in front of the mirror to learn how to spell, guys?

www.beautifulpeople.net (£14.95 a month) claims to be 'the most beautiful and coveted network in the UK. A focused way of seeking and finding likeminded people of a similar social standing and physical appearance.' To join you submit yourself to a Big-Brother-style vote, with members deciding if your photo is fit to grace the same pages as these self-appointed lovelies. If your idea of a potential mate is a catalogue model nicknamed Cupcake, or a shiny-toothed preppy called Yoghurtmaker, throw yourself to their mercy. Those of us whose gene pool is only half full can avoid the humiliation of being told that 'BeautifulPeople.net did not find your application attractive enough to grant you membership.'

Pets win partners

Love me, love my dog – or in this case, date me, date my pet – is the motto of some love surfers. The defining aspect of their life is their pet, and their partner needs to share their adoration.

www.horseloversconnection.com ($20 a month) announces itself as a dating service 'where single horse people find friendship, romance and love'. Daters are divided into English or Western riding styles, and though the site is mostly populated by North Americans, a fair number of UK daters step into the saddle here. So if you are looking for a home on the range with a hunky cowboy/girl, why not blaze a trail here? It's a friendly, if not literate, place – as this dater's story shows: 'i met the most hansom cowboy my life, i drove 3 days and 2 nights to meet him. we clicked at once, and i lived with him. i was realy happy with him – and he also with me. We fall for each other and he is my friend forever in my hearth.'

www.kissykat.com ($14.65 a month) tags itself as the place 'where people who love their pets find love'. Members vary from liberal professionals who are animal advocates, to 35-year-old Puss-in-Boots from Croydon who describes herself as 'a cat mad lady looking for a cat mad man'.

Love sports

Regular dating sites are full of profiles recounting tales of derring-do. The monocycled-across-the-Gobi-desert type person would often be better suited to a sports/hobby-orientated site such as

www.newfriends4u.com. If you want to ice skate with Tracy from Chelmsford, bungee jump with Bill from Bradford, or ballroom dance with Kate from Kilmarnock, then try this UK-run site (£15.95 a month).

Swimmers in search of love head for **www.poolpull.com** – a funky little site whose motto is 'Dive right in and find your perfect match' – and, rather charmingly, you can do this for free.

www.bikerdating.co.uk (£10 for lifetime membership) is for you if you like tearing down the highway on a Harley in search of crop circles. Daters here seem to like a mix of grunge and new-age philosophy; a good balance of biker chicks and rocky road boys.

Disabled dating

www.whispers4u.com (W: free, M seeking W: £4.99) promotes itself as 'a dating site for disabled singles, handicapped or amputees'. The site is international, featuring a strong mix of UK and Australian daters, with disabilities from MS to visual impairment.

www.lovebyrd.com is a free US-based site for 'adults who live with physical, mental and emotional disabilities, medical conditions and challenges in life'. Members' 'disabilities' vary: from social phobia to cerebral palsy. It's a well-run, professional-looking site with a reasonable selection of international members.

www.cupidcalls.co.uk – Cupid Calls (free) describes itself as 'an "all inclusive" website where people from all walks of life can interact and find love. We proactively seek membership from all sections of the community – especially disabled people.'

Believe in love

For many, faith is the defining factor of a relationship – they want a partner who worships the same way they do. All the major religions have dating sites.

www.bigchurch.com ($19.95 per month) promotes itself as 'bringing people together in love and faith', with search options to find partners for 'bible study' or 'prayer' dates. A big church it is indeed, romancing Christian denominations from the Amish to a faith called Two by Twos. 'Love Him, Love me', says Emma from Surrey, while Jenny from Jedburgh's tag line is 'find me a mate god'. For those with a knowledge of scripture, you can run a partner search based on a favourite passage from the Bible.

www.jdate.com ($18 for one month) is the world's largest Jewish singles network. Members are 'a high-quality group of singles from all walks of life, professions and ages'. However, the majority boast a pedigree which includes 'a professional degree and an average income exceeding $60,000 a year. One out of every ten UK Jewish singles is on our site with a 50/50 male to female ratio.' Jewish mothers breathe a sigh of relief! This online equivalent of a social club is full of eligible high-achieving men and women. The good news (and the bad news) is that 'everybody knows everybody' (either directly or by association). Jewish singles like it, and tend not to stray (into goy pastures new) because they feel comfortable here. A recent face-lift has brought Jdate into the 21st century with hot-lists and 'teases'.

www.twomuslims.co.uk is a free site for UK Muslims. Its philosophy is 'faith, love and community'. The significance of 'two' is revealed by their statement: 'We cannot accept requests for second wives as polygamy is illegal by our national laws.' **www.greatcompanion.com** ($7 a month) 'provides halal, safe, and honourable' Muslim matchmaking.

Love for sale?

In the world of internet romance, a man in possession of a good fortune (and the right passport) is every Russian bride's dream. This kind of dating is now so popular that the phrase 'Russian bride' is now in the dictionary. It is, however, totally different from the dating discussed in this chapter, in that it's about the meeting of opposites.

There are hundreds of online agencies in the former Soviet bloc offering thousands of beautiful women apparently desperate to meet a man who speaks a different language, lives thousands of miles away and, presumably, can't get a date in his home town.

Online agencies specialising in Russian and Eastern European women boast that this is the way for Western men to find beautiful, well-educated women who are prepared to date them. It all takes place in an atmosphere oblivious to the consequences of late-20th-century feminism, with most women casting themselves as 1950s housewives – eager to welcome their man back home from a hard day at the office.

What is also obvious, and well documented, is that there are some unscrupulous people out there waiting to scam you out of your money – you should approach these agencies with the same caution you would a second-hand car salesman. Do a search on the net to research any agency you are thinking of handing money over to, adding in the word 'scam', 'phony' or 'rip off' to see if anybody has been stung by the site.

A Foreign Affair (at www.loveme.com) has thousands of profiles of women from the former Soviet Union. Dating is more like shopping here. There are no serious search facilities, but a massive photo catalogue of Elanas, Olgas and Svetlanas all seemingly in search of a 'sincere and loving partner with good manners'.

If you want to speak to them you will have to buy addresses (postal or email) at about £5 each. Alternatively you can join a romance tour, costing from £2,000, where you fly out on a holiday and are taken to several parties to meet potential mates.

www.luckylovers.net claims it is an 'easy efficient honest way to meet singles and find a dream date'. With over 100,000 members, it is free for women to join but men have to pay. Many profile descriptions feel like Hallmark card ditties: 36-year-old Princess from the Ukraine is 'extremely attractive, both in face and body. She has a very sweet, soft and high voice and a man would melt to hear voice say sweet loving things to him.' It's a bit unfair to mock, as most of us would struggle to write a profile in another language – and the women are better educated than many of the matches they are likely to find – but there is something slightly surreal about Russian bride hunting.

Tangled web

The words cyber and sex, it seems, are the perfect match. Google search 'adult internet dating', and you get over a million hits, from the dubious to the pornographic. Some are simply a way of scamming a membership fee from you, so do a bit of research before you hand over money to a site you know nothing about.

There are several well-run sites for men and women who are looking for a sexual encounter. The best known is **www.adultfriendfinder.com** ($19.95 a month), which promotes itself as the 'world's largest sex and swinger personals site' with over 12 million active members. Many of these 'members' feature on a photo site – frequently resembling outtakes from bad porn flicks. The site has online chat, home video exchange and discussion groups, with debates on pressing questions such as 'dildo or dick?' and 'are Kentish women prudes?'.

www.sexintheuk.com (£14.99 a month – free for women and couples) is a UK-based site for adult encounters, with 250,000 users. 'We're an offshoot of the regular dating site Date the UK', explains director Fiona Maclean. 'Every Friday night, men would come home from the pub, log on to Date the UK and start sending explicit chat messages. The unwilling women recipients would either close their account, or complain. In response we set up Sex in the UK, and told the men that if they wanted sex talk, this was the right place for it. Like most adult sites, there's one woman for every ten men. We don't charge women to join; some men try to get round this by posing as women – they are soon found out.' Sex in the UK is less pornographic than other adult sites. The signature photography is arty black and white, and there are some relatively demure tag lines: 'Rubenesque novice submissive seeks intelligent and caring dominant', says Tigerblossom from Edinburgh, while DealBoy asks women to 'come and join me in pleasure pleasure land'. Deal in Kent? Pleasureland?

www.alt.com ($35.97 for three months) pitches itself as the 'World's Largest BDSM & Alternative Lifestyle Personals'. For the uninitiated the acronym 'BDSM' is 'B&D' (Bondage and Discipline), 'D&S' (Dominance and Submission), 'S&M' (sadomasochism) and a kaleidoscope of other sexual customs. Alt.com's search list of activities sends you scuttling for a dictionary: for example, podophilia (foot fetish), retifism (that's feet again, but this time clad), and klismaphilia (look it up, if you *really* want to know). Other more plain-English practices include 'nunplay', 'medieval devices', 'feathers' and – in a throwback to the school playground – 'doctors and nurses'. Members can also post webcam videos, the jerky way these 'erotic videos' are streamed makes them more an internet what-the-butler-saw than *Emmanuelle*.

Chapter 6

YOU'VE GOT MAIL

The Art of E-Flirting

The hope that there is someone 'out there' for each of us is heightened a hundred-fold in cyberspace where any number of suitors could be waiting to meet us.

And their way of making contact? The email. Anticipating the arrival of that one, elusive missive on the cyber mat is what makes internet dating so compelling.

It's also what makes us part with our money. Dating sites are all too aware of this, and most won't let you send or read emails until you've become a fully paid-up member. They bombard you with messages saying 'You've got mail', knowing that as soon as somebody you like the look of makes contact, you'll have your credit card out in a flash.

Even the most miserly of daters eventually succumb to the lure of a bulging inbox. But reading mail can be a huge anti-climax.

❝*I joined Dating Direct because one particular girl emailed me. She was so stunning, I didn't even read her profile. But as soon as I opened her mail, and saw:'Us sexi scorpios have got to stik togetha' – I felt like a fool.* **❞**

Dave

On some sites non-subscribers can't view the profiles of people who have contacted them. But if a sufficient number of people email you, it's hard to resist having a look in the hope that one or two will make it worth your while.

66When I first joined Udate, I wasn't sure if I wanted to subscribe but when I saw the 'You've got mail' icon winking at me for the 35th time … my curiosity got the better of me and I 'succumbed'. Sadly all 35 men were really awful so it was a complete let-down. 99

Celia

A way to woo

Some people see internet dating as a welcome return to a more romantic era when literary loving was the way to woo. Fancying themselves as a latter-day Austen or Pepys, they relish seduction by mail. For others, having to write prose brings on feelings of unworthiness they haven't experienced since school.

But whoever you are, the dilemma is essentially the same: how do you write an appealing message to someone you've never met? You can have the best profile in the world – written with painstaking honesty and charm – but if you can't give good email, your great profile is about as useful as a corkscrew at an AA meeting.

Making the first move

What happens once you've posted a winning profile, and uploaded a decent mugshot? For women, it can be a case of sitting back and watching the mail pile in. Men, meanwhile, may have to try a bit harder.

Some women receive so much mail when their profile goes

live that they don't have the time, or need, to contact people themselves.

Meanwhile there are other women, such as Julia from Love and Friends, who believe the man should take the lead: 'I might send a "wink" or something. But I won't ask for a date. I am still old-fashioned. I want a man to be a man.'

But, male or female, the majority of daters prefer to take a back-seat approach. Three-quarters of the people we surveyed refuse to make the first move. Most of them put this down to the sense of rejection they feel when they don't get a reply. But they are forgetting a major advantage of online dating – its anonymity. Making contact online is much less daunting than in 'real life', as Swoozi from Love and Friends points out. 'The brilliant thing about this medium is that it's much easier to take rejection. I would never approach a man in a bar, but I have contacted people on dating sites. It's cool because the person can just say "no thanks" and you never have to face them!'

And women like Sarah from Dating Direct relish the opportunity to be more direct. 'In the outside world I would never make the first move. Online it's so liberating – you can chat up as many men as you like. I love the power reversal.'

So, step forward, dating wallflowers. As well as the freedom initiating contact brings, you are much more likely to find the right partner this way than by leaving it to chance and the hope that Mr or Ms Right will pluck you from the crowd.

Breaking the ice

So what is the fastest way into a person's inbox? The advice offered by some of the sites is lame. Udate urges you to: 'Say something fascinating about yourself!' But if you haven't already said something fascinating about yourself in your profile it's a bit late now.

What it should say is: 'Say something interesting about the person you're writing to.' After all, it's them you're flirting with, not yourself. Attracting people online is not so different from flirting in the real world: you have to compliment and 'include' people. Don't use it as an opportunity to talk about yourself – if someone introduced themselves at a party by saying: 'I've got a black belt in karate and I speak fluent Mandarin', it would be frightening rather than a cue for a conversation.

As Sandra from Match says: 'What I can't understand is why so many perfectly intelligent men seem to lose it on a dating site, forgetting the rules of seduction.'

The best way to attract someone's attention is to look at their profile, find something you can comment on and start a conversation. So rather than sending a one-liner saying, 'I love Eddie Izzard too', try 'Did you see him on *Parkinson* last week? What did you think?'

This approach works even better if you can do it with humour – the key to many a person's heart, as Karen from Snog London confirms: 'Humour is everything. If a man makes me laugh (and doesn't have a face like a bag of spanners) – I'm there like a shot.'

Men appreciate humour: they also appreciate being contacted at all.

" *If you can write well and you're funny, men are so flattered by the attention, they get pulled in immediately. Either that, or they're just pleased to get mail.* **"**

'Butseriously', Soulmates

" *I will almost always write back to a woman who contacts me first because it's such a nice surprise. Even if she's not exactly my type, if she gives good email, she can win me over straight away!* **"**

Kevin, Love and Friends

Some people are masters at e-flirting

I can see I'm going to have to work a little harder at this but don't worry, persuading a woman to date me against her will is one of my particular talents.

You probably didn't reply to my message because you're too busy having nights in with a video and a bottle of wine. Or, flushed with enthusiasm by the new series of *Sex and the City*, you're out buying this season's Manolos.

I guess really you've just had more than one message from nice boys, you've had to prioritise and I just missed the cut. I have therefore commissioned a report from Lord Hutton which emphasises a few of the positive points that put me above your run-of-the-mill online date prospects.

Here's the executive summary:

a) I'm single in real life, not just in my imagination

b) I am dead intelligent – you would never find the *Sun* in my bathroom and I have never read John Grisham

c) I am also dead classy. Last month alone I went to the Opera in Prague and cooked ricotta gnocchi

d) I don't go on about myself all the time

e) I'm a catch, goddamn it. At least do me the courtesy of telling me to piss off and leave you alone!

All the other women on the site look rubbish. I would really like to speak to you. Ah, go on, go on, go on, go on, go on …

You know who you are.

Fishing for favourites

If you are feeling shy or you're a novice who wants to test the water, you can always employ the 'friends' or 'favourites' tool offered by most sites to coax people into action. The idea is that you earmark someone as a favourite and if they return the compliment, you know you have a green light to make a move.

Sites usually offer you ice-breakers such as 'one-liners' or 'winks' that you can send online. But it's worth remembering that not everybody enjoys this approach, like one dater on Love and Friends: 'It annoys me when I get winked at in the street, so why should I like it online?'

What not to write

So much is revealed by what you include, or fail to include, in an opening email. Get it wrong – or, more to the point, *keep* getting it wrong – and the lack of replies could put you off internet dating for good.

Knowing what to say to someone shouldn't be difficult – most profiles put an arsenal of information at your fingertips. Yet many opening gambits suggest daters don't think before they hit 'send' (see box).

No-hopers

I.

Get yourself an Italian latte and take time to savour every sip whilst slowly reading my tantalising response to your advert.

I am Alan and am 30 years old, 5ft 8in, slim build from Edinburgh where I have been brought up. I am living in the bright lights of London due to my work.

Trendy, elegant, reliable, good to look at. Funsome, warm-hearted and cuddly. Yep, that's my cat all right. But me too! – and more: personable with heart of gold, good-looking, curves in all the very right places, funny and very witty. Well, if I were a mobile phone I would be described as trendy, elegant, robust, reliable, good to look at and user-friendly.

All you need to have is the 3 C's. Just in-case your thinking what they might be, it's simple chemistry, communication and commitment; and not charm, curves and cash as people keep on telling me.

If you are interested drop me a line.

2.

Hi
I see you're a poet too.
See if you can decipher this code: URAQT
Alan

3.

I've selected you because you are the only person on the site who doesn't look entirely like an axe-wielding murderer.

If you are as intelligent and 'comfortable' as you claim in your profile, perhaps you'd like to write to me and tell me about your career and why you have ended up on a site like this.
Yours, Sapphire

4.

Oops, no photo as I am a techno luddite and don't own a camera. So let me describe what I look like. I'm not Adonis, just an ordinary bloke. Will try and get round to a photo and work out how to load on this website if you insist. Or send it by post to your work address, as I know I can manage that.

I am serious, genuine, looking for a soulmate and I can bear soul but don't take me to a jazz club – can't stand discordant music. You can go, I won't stop you, but please don't take me.

So, look at the profile (gosh, dating by numbers and statistics is so much fun, NOT) and if I am worthy of a quick coffee in between films please let me know. Are you A or B films? Where do you see yourself in the next five years? So many questions! Give me a call drop me a line or even email me. I'm a post and telephone – not an email person.

5.

Hi

Okay, so I live 9 hours from Gatwick Airport, if I don't use the Concorde ha ha ha ;) ;) a small pond is all that keeps us aprat … I was in Stratford upon Avon and Oxford last summer. Oh, look out, I love to cook, I cook a lot of different types of food. Mornings, I like either an English breakfast or a breakfast pizza grilled out on the deck.

I am a writer. Ok so I have only one book out, working on my next now. My book did ok in England but better in Wales. I like to walk in the country side and in parks. I am 40 years young and love com shows. I like So Graham Norton and I like Changing Rooms and EastEnders. Also Manchester United and F1 racing.

I love plays. I would like to find a soulmate, someone to grow older with, not old. I write down names like Steven & Susan and ask does it fit?

Yeah it does go together nice. Maybe you have read my book?

Hope to hear from you.

6.

I have booked a table for two at Nobu on Saturday night. If you're man enough to come, tell me what you'd wear, what you'd order and how you'd get me home. (Lady P)

The number one offence is spam – a scattergun approach to emailing that works on the basis that if you send out twenty messages, one recipient will 'bite'. But as Toby from Udate points out, 'If your opening email is off a production line it's hardly going to attract someone's attention.'

The email equivalent of 'Do you come here often?', these identikit messages range from the short 'I like your profile – have a look at mine' – which translates as 'Yours is okay, but hey, mine's even better' – to the rambling 'standard' email which usually runs to several, dull paragraphs. This might as well read: 'I've never pulled anyone in my life and probably never will', it's so off-message. It's also spotted a mile off (see box overleaf).

Sometimes the author's only attempt to 'personalise' their one-message-fits-all mail is to include your name at the top. If they are feeling particularly creative they may stretch to one sentence that relates to you. To stop people from spamming, some sites limit the number of emails a member can send in one day. Others, such as Snog London, send emailed warnings if their systems detect spam.

Another excruciating first email is the 'Hi x, how are you to-day?' message. Karen says: 'I never, ever, reply – these men! They don't seem to get that they're not in a bar/pub/club/party.' Caroline agrees: 'It's bad enough when you're walking down the street and some builder says it, but online it's just ridiculous – not to men-tion lazy.'

It's not just men who lack imagination. Some female attempts fall flat too. 'Some women seem hellbent on finding a sugar daddy', says Andrew from Love and Friends. 'They say they want some-one to spoil them and ask you what you'd buy them for Christmas.'

And there are some women who think they can skip social niceties, and launch a full-blown attack. 'If someone sends you an email full of criticism and negativity, you're not likely to think "Ah!

The 'standard' email

Hi there.

A bit about me.

Born in Yorkshire, I moved to London to take my maths degree and stayed for 13 years. I then fled to East Anglia on a 7-year contract and have been here ever since! I was, until recently, a Software Architect, but my love of Tai Chi led me to a life change and I'm now training to be a psychotherapist in my spare time.

I have varied interests from boats – I'm building a canoe in the back garden – to mountain climbing. I'm hoping to visit the Atlas Mountains this Summer. I'm also a keen golfer and I play badminton. Holiday-wise, I try to make a great escape every year. Last year was Chile, this year China beckons!

I'm a passable cook and can make a mean tortilla. There's nothing I like more than having a bunch of friends over on a Saturday night altho' I sometimes regret it on Sundays!

If you like what you read, drop me a line.

You sound interesting.

Steve

Sweet mystery of life! At last I've found you!'", says Max from Love and Friends.

Overtly sexual emails are another cause for complaint, as well as those in which the man (usually) asks to meet you straight away, or gives you his phone number. (Their profiles are almost always unaccompanied by a photograph, which suggests they're married.)

As Penny from Snog London says: 'The worst are the people who send you: "Wow, ur gorgeous – here's my number, call me", or "Would you like to meet up for a drink?" on a first email! Purlease … like that's really gonna happen. No wonder they're single!'

Strangely enough this is not merely a female issue – quite a few men complain that women sometimes steer things in a sexual direction. Mike from Udate says: 'On a couple of occasions I have received instant messages from women telling me exactly what they want to do with me. It's quite scary.'

The volume of sexmail can depend on the site – a quick scan of user names will often provide a clue. If there are an inordinate number of 4play69s or rampantrabbits, chances are their mail will not mince its words.

Some sites have built-in software that filters out mail with a strong sexual content; they also freeze profiles if the person continues to offend.

Next!

"If I feel that men write to me without even reading my profile, that annoys me. Also if, in their message, they repeat the same thing about themselves as is in their profile.**"**

Katherine, Udate

"The 'Hey babe how you doin'?' emails: the online incarnation of medallion man.**"**

Karen, Yahoo Personals

"People who can't spell! There are so many illiterates out 'their' – (joke). Am also driven mad by 'lol' … grrr. Badly written mails are a complete turn off for me.**"**

Liz, Snog London

❝I don't like mails which don't tell you why a person was interested in your profile. And anyone calling me sexy and gorgeous in any mail, let alone in the first, will never get a reply. **❞**

Martina, Match

❝People who ask to meet in the first email. **❞**

Caroline, Snog London

❝People who email you with an air of arrogance, implying that you should feel special that they chose YOU to email. **❞**

Samuel, Match

❝The worst by a LONG, LONG way is: 'Hi my name is John, I am 33 married with 2 kids. I am looking for discreet adult fun in hotels in and around the Victoria area …' **❞**

Petra, Udate

❝Men who take it upon themselves to pull your profile to pieces e.g. 'How can you like Chilean merlot, French is so much better!' **❞**

Coco, Love and Friends

❝The ones that say: 'I'm sure you've had hundreds of emails from men much better-looking than me …' Self-deprecation has its place and it's not in an opening email! Humour is the way to a girl's heart (and other places a lack of self-confidence doesn't reach). **❞**

Helen, Friends Reunited Dating

Opening gambit dos and don'ts – a round-up

Do
1. Think about what you want to say
2. Say something about the other person's profile, i.e. things you have in common or things which impressed you
3. Be funny (i.e. prove that you are)
4. Be friendly (you haven't got facial expressions to help you get away with irony)
5. Be flattering (but not cheesy)
6. If you say 'I like your profile', say why
7. Avoid cliché

Don't
1. Send a cut-and-paste 'standard' email – you can spot them a mile off
2. Employ dodgy one-liners (they don't work in the outside world; they work even less well 'in the dark')
3. Say 'I like your profile, have a look at mine' – it's boring, not to mention lazy … and arrogant
4. Put yourself down, for example, 'If my photo hasn't made you run a mile, pls write back' (unless it's funny)
5. Be overly apologetic – 'I hope you don't mind me disturbing you' – you're on a dating site for god's sake!
6. Just say 'We have a lot in common' or 'I think we'd get on'
7. Immediately suggest meeting up or give them your phone number
8. (Women) Give too much away … or be overtly sexual – it's one thing to be 'liberated' but maybe not in an opening email
9. Write too much (even if it's tailor-made for them) – they don't need your life story

To reply or not to reply

It's one thing to compose mail but how do you go about answering it – especially when you're not interested in the person it's from?

Internet daters tend to fall into one of three camps: those who always reply; those who never reply; and those who reply only when the sender has clearly made an effort. (The subject provokes very strong reactions, as any discussion on dating site forums will testify.)

Many dating sites advise sending a response to every message even if just to say 'thanks, but no thanks'. Some have ready-made one-liners which do the work for you such as 'thanks, but I don't think we're right for one another', or 'I think our age difference would be too large' (Soulmates).

The silent treatment

There is, however, an unwritten rule among daters that says ignoring people is fine. Many people think it's the kindest response: 'Telling people I don't find them attractive is surely far worse than ignoring them', says Karen.

Sally from Kiss agrees: 'The one time I did get an email from a man saying "Sorry, I don't find you attractive", I was so upset I wrote to him and advised him to ignore someone next time: it's much kinder.'

Daters who employ a strict no-reply policy cite another reason: it leaves no room for confusion. 'If you send a "thanks for your mail" reply', says Alice, 'it will often elicit another email – getting you nowhere.'

Robert echoes this: 'What tends to happen then is you've started a dialogue you didn't mean to start. At some point you'll have to end it anyway.'

Replying to every message is also hugely impractical for those people – usually women – who receive a high volume of mail.

Fifi from Love and Friends says: 'I don't have time to answer every email. I have a life outside the internet.' Rebecca from Yahoo Personals agrees: 'If I answered every mail I get, it would be a full-time job!'

Thanks but no thanks

But if you do think it's important to respond to 'unwanted' mail, how do you go about it? Spelling out in no uncertain terms that you don't find the sender attractive doesn't come naturally to most of us.

The 'little white lie' is the online dater's let-down of choice, and, so it seems, that of the sites themselves. One of the automatic responses on Soulmates, for example, is 'thanks, but I think I've already met my match here'.

The problem with this is that the 'transparent' nature of most sites – you can see when people log on – means you'll invariably get found out, thereby upsetting the very person you set out to 'protect'.

❝I hate it when men say 'Sorry, I've already found someone' but every time you log on their profile is still there. It makes me want to send them a sarcastic message saying, 'Lucky girl!' ❞

Sarah, Dating Direct

Probably the best bet is to say: 'I'm afraid you're not really what I'm looking for, but I wish you every success.'

Going quietly

Whether you reply or not, neither policy guarantees that your admirer will accept defeat gracefully. A minority of daters cannot abide being ignored and will write again to let you know.

❝ *They usually start with innocuous messages like 'I don't bite!' then move on to 'You could at least have the decency to acknowledge my existence', and finish up with 'You're not that pretty anyway'.* **❞**

Rebecca, Dating Direct

In the worst cases, disgruntled daters register their disapproval by 'blocking' you so you can't contact them again. This can mean that you can suddenly find yourself being warned (or even have your profile deleted) by the site, effectively for being too polite.

Alison from Faceparty says she's changed her replying tactics because of this. 'I used to reply to everyone but a lot of the weirdos would get the hump that I'd politely declined, and block me. Block *me*! As if I ever wanted to speak to them in the first place! I ended up getting a warning from the site when I was just trying to do the right thing.'

A handful of daters insist on knowing why you're not interested or become abusive. Luckily these are few and far between.

Our advice, again, is to treat online dating as you would face-to-face dating. As Jane from Yahoo Personals says, 'Just because someone makes contact with you in a bar does not mean you have to thank them for it.'

Email relationships

So once you've got over the initial hurdle of making contact, what happens next?

Email 'relationships' can take many forms. Some start with a bang and then go out with a whimper within the space of a few days. Others get off to a shaky start, with both of you fielding for interesting topics, but improve once you've hit a mutual spot. And then there are those that are so compelling from the word go that you spend several hours feverishly emailing one another before arranging to meet the next day.

The beauty of online dating is that you can take relationships at your own pace. If someone starts to hint that you're not answering fast enough with the odd 'You've gone very quiet' line or 'Cat got your tongue?' and it bothers you, you can ignore them. Don't let anybody pressurise you into moving things along more quickly than you're happy with. If someone suggests chatting on the phone or meeting and it seems too soon, say so. If they object, you have your answer anyway.

By far the best scenario is when you establish a connection with someone and a natural flirtation ensues.

"I love the verbal sparring – sometimes all made up of one-liners – where you just play with words, like you would do at a party. You never actually go down the 'What do you do for a living?' route. It's so exciting because you never know how long it will be before they say 'Well, come on then, what's your phone number?'**"**

Karen

"My favourites are those that start as quick but regular messages where we exchange nothing more than witticisms and nonsensical one-liners. One time we spent a whole week discussing our favourite proper nouns. His was Cirencester!**"**

Stacy, Udate

However, for email relationships to 'take off', there has to be some discernible progression. Otherwise email 'rot' sets in.

As Dave from Udate says: 'Some get off to a good start. Nice girl, intelligent, all good on paper – but after an exchange of emails you realise this is all very nice – but there's no flirting and it starts to feel more of a chore like writing thank you letters at Christmas. These go: "So what did you do today? How was your w/e?" and … don't go any further.'

And sometimes signals you didn't pick up on at the off become apparent as the dialogue progresses. This can often happen when you've been swayed by a person's picture and are flattered they made contact.

'I was taken in by this "babe" (sorry) on Snog London but then her copious use of "lol" and references to reality TV started to grate', says one dater.

The best is yet to come

Romancing by email has many advantages. For a start, you can do it from the comfort of your own home – 'dressed in your pyjamas with no make-up on and greasy hair', as one convert puts it.

For the backward in coming forward, it can be a godsend – ruling out painful 'cold' meetings with total strangers. It's a great way for isolated people to 'get out more', without having to pay babysitters or travel for hours.

Internet dating is undoubtedly a cool, and efficient, way of locating other single people and getting to know them gradually online. But the moment of truth – seeing what your virtual mate is like in real life – can happen only on a date.

Chapter 7

DATE EXPECTATIONS

The First Meeting

Reality bytes

So you've exchanged the email and text messages, but when is the right time to meet? Our answer is unequivocal: sooner rather than later. Why? Because some people are very good at writing – but their live appearance leaves you cold.

An email can include clever quotes, your best jokes, a cunningly cut-and-pasted love poem – all re-worked until your message displays the wisdom of Wilde. But – unlike an email – a date can't be deleted, as Martina from Love and Friends discovered: 'I loved this guy on email. He was smart and funny, only to be a mouse upon meeting. I had to drag words out of him.'

The telephone is a more reliable indicator of personality: 'The sooner you talk on the phone,' says Jane from Match, 'the sooner you can get internet dating into the realms of "reality".' Though you might want to wait a bit longer than Susan from Soulmates: 'I phoned him before I knew his real name. When this guy answered the phone I had to ask "Is that … um … Sensualcreative?" – turned out I was talking to his flatmate.'

The spontaneity of the phone gives you a more realistic picture of a potential date. 'I always speak before meeting, to see if the conversation flows freely', says Matt from Match. 'There is nothing worse than sitting in a pub or restaurant with nothing to say.'

Some people have a natural advantage on the phone. 'Voice is important to me', says Ben from Snog London. 'In many ways it's more important than looks. I am a big fan of a woman with a sexy voice or exotic accent.' Kevin from Match has a similar weakness: 'I was completely blown away by a very husky, sexy northern accent. I kept chatting to her on the phone, simply because I didn't want her to hang up – it was heaven. Sadly the date was rubbish – she didn't fancy me a bit.'

Kelly from Love and Friends had what she called an 'aural fixation'. 'I talked to one guy for so long on the phone that by the time we met I had practically fallen in love with him – or I should say his voice. When he sloped up to me at Waterloo station in a Disney-themed baseball cap my heart sunk. I tried to recreate the feeling during the date by closing my eyes so I could just hear his voice – it worked until he asked me what was going on!'

Unfortunately, if there is a Sean Connery effect, there's a David Beckham one too: 'I phoned this guy who had a terrible, terrible Essex accent', says Liz from Snog London. 'It was so high-pitched, it sounded as if he was being fast-forwarded inside a dustbin. I couldn't bring myself to speak to him again.'

Of course unappealing voices aren't always to blame for an aural anti-climax: it might be what they say that grates, as Karen from Yahoo Personals describes. 'There was one guy I now call Cliché Man. The whole conversation was punctuated with "at the end of the day", "it's all swings and roundabouts", and "what goes around comes around". I just knew I'd kill him if we went on a date.'

The advantage of calling someone is that it gives you the chance to pull out of a date if someone's phone persona puts you off. Marina from Snog London learned this from experience:

Phone disasters

❝I called one woman, and the entire conversation was punctuated with her son shouting 'dickhead' in the background. Despite her denials, it was obvious her son was aiming his remarks at me.**❞**

Brian

❝I used to play rugby, and when I started speaking about it to one internet dater, she confessed that it made her feel sexy. This got me a little turned on, and we ended up having great phone sex. This went on every day for a week, but when I asked her if we should meet up, she said she couldn't because in truth we didn't really know each other and there would be too much pressure on us to end up shagging.**❞**

Matt

❝A guy from Udate called me. Rather than have a polite chat, he wanted to know if I was interested in going to live with him in Spain. Apparently he was only in the UK for a few days and had to find a woman before he left and take her with him.**❞**

Elaine

❝Met a lovely girl online then spoke on the phone to find that she ended every sentence with 'you know what I mean?' I'm sure she remains a lovely girl but I just kept thinking I was Harry Carpenter to her Frank Bruno.**❞**

Forlorn Hope, Love and Friends

❝I met two men, both called John. One day they called at the same time: one on the land line, the other on the mobile. My children answered, and simultaneously shouted: 'It's your date, John.' I was praying the two Johns hadn't overheard.**❞**

PamelaAnn, My UK Date

'If a guy called, I would always meet him. Then I went on a date with someone who had told me over the phone that he had only just broken up with his ex. He went on and on about her. Now I am more experienced and make excuses if I hear negative signs.'

All good reasons to have a Plan B up your sleeve. Martin from Jdate always has a get-out clause ready if a phone call puts him off. 'I just say I'm going away on business for a couple of weeks and that I'll be in touch when I get back.'

Another reason to meet quickly is to stop your imagination running wild. A nice picture, a glowing profile, some heavy emailing, and you can soon develop a warm and fuzzy feeling about someone as your imagination fills in any information you don't have. And because fantasy is much better than reality – otherwise what would be the point of it – you invent your perfect match. 'It's like reading a book, then seeing the movie', as Liz from Love and Friends puts it. 'The film is often disappointing because it's not what you had in mind.'

Before you know it, you're smitten with someone you've never met. Over half the people in our survey confess to having fallen in love with people before they met. No doubt this 'virtual love syndrome' will give birth to hundreds of support groups in the future. But spare yourself the agony of falling for a flawless person you've invented and don't expect your dates to live up to an image in your head.

Another reason to get up close with a potential match is chemistry. The intangible element that brings lovers together and sustains a relationship can be experienced only when they are in the same place; the sooner you find out if you have – or don't have – this, the better.

Should you meet everybody?

In the first flush of internet dating, some people rush out to meet everybody they make contact with – they soon learn to be selective. If you can't find enough to talk about over the phone, imagine being in a situation where you can't escape from them by claiming you need to feed the cat.

It's tiring meeting people for the first time. If you're active on several dating sites, you could easily meet two or three people a week. Recounting the same sparkling stories night after night is not natural, and many daters report 'internet-dating fatigue' – they can't summon up the energy and enthusiasm to meet another date. The way to avoid this is to meet only those that really interest you – don't let yourself get to the stage where you meet people as a matter of routine.

Dating nerves

Life is not like *Groundhog Day* – there is no rehearsal. We all care about what other people think of us, even if we see them only once. So a first date can be nerve-wracking. Some people are so traumatised by the idea of a physical meeting that they spend months and months online, finding out more and more about people, but never committing to a real-life encounter.

❝I spent six months online, exchanging emails, chatting to men on the phone. Then I would arrange to meet them, and cancel the day before. Most men would lose patience, but there's one guy I've been chatting to for over a year now. We live 2 miles apart, but have never met – it's the internet date for eternity. **❞**

Kelly, Udate

❝ I started exchanging emails online. The relationship on text and email got more and more intense. But we both work shifts, and couldn't find a convenient time to meet. Then we both went on holiday. All the time we were texting, emailing, chatting on the phone. He was ill, and I kept in touch with him, I was having problems at work, he was supportive. This went on for 2 months, then suddenly the emails got cooler until they just stopped. It was bizarre, like a relationship with a beginning, middle and end, but never meeting someone. **❞**

Val, Love and Friends

Overcoming dating nerves

Everybody finds the idea of sitting across the table from a stranger who might become their partner disconcerting. So try to view it objectively. Pitch your anxiety against the reality of the situation by reminding yourself that there are three possible outcomes to an internet date:

1. You spend an hour or so chatting to somebody you would not want as a friend or lover
2. You really hit it off with someone, and would like to be friends with them, but there is no 'chemistry'
3. You hit it off, and they are a potential girlfriend or boyfriend

We can all afford half an hour passed with someone who is not our perfect match. In the grand scheme of things, it's no big deal. If you simply can't face a one-to-one encounter, you can always contrive some other way to meet people. One woman from Love and Friends invited all her potential dates to a big house party. This worked on several levels. 'My friends got to give them the once-over, but, more importantly, I could say I'd met my boyfriend at a party, and not online!'

Watch out for people that really aren't prepared to meet. There are telltale signs: if, after a couple of weeks, someone refuses to speak on the phone, or constantly postpones meetings, the reality of a real-life date may simply be too much for them. Nearly half the people we spoke to in our survey with My UK Date said that they were 'addicted' to chatting online.

Where to meet?

Fortunately the mobile phone means that the 'pink carnation' is no longer needed to track down a blind date. Even so, don't arrange to meet in a teemingly busy place – it's hard enough trying to identify the person you have only seen in a pixelated picture, without having to pick them out from the rush-hour crowd.

One of the less inspiring profile questions on the Udate site is: 'Where is the best place to go on a date?' The women's responses include several fantasies, the most popular being the 'We'll-always-have-Paris' date where you romance with potential paramours in Florence/San Francisco/Barcelona/A.N. other amorous city. Other favourites are: 'on a beach, the waves lapping on the shore' and 'sipping red wine in front of a roaring log fire'. As Jackie from Love and Friends says, 'The log fire bit! What's that about? For goodness sake this is England. We all have central heating.'

The fantasy dates are fine on the good ship Barbara Cartland, but do you really want to be stuck with someone you have never met before on a far-away island? The only sensible answer to the where to meet question is 'somewhere quiet where we can talk' (the response given by most of Udate's pragmatic men). This still leaves you with a lot of choice, as Matt from Love and Friends points out: 'I have met people at the zoo, a museum, an airport, a train station and a school (don't worry, she was a teacher) but I am most comfortable in a quiet bar. There is something to refer to if there is conversational silence, but you can still hear the other person talk.' And Gill from My UK Date says: 'I often meet in an art gallery, or museum – it gives you something to talk about, and helps take the pressure off.'

The first meeting with an internet date needs a degree of freedom. The freedom to talk – best avoid cinema or theatre – and the freedom to leave after an acceptable period of time if the date is not going well. Choose a quiet place, where you can chat, and make a dignified and safe exit if you don't hit it off. An early evening drink is a good idea. That way, if you find you're not getting along, you can leave without embarrassment because 'early evening' implies that you have something to do later on. On the other hand, if the date is going well, you can simply carry on enjoying yourself.

Avoid arranging a three-course dinner, or a day trip to Brighton. By definition these will last for hours – the only way out being a drastic lie, where you almost have to fake your own death.

❝I met a date for a Chinese meal. I'd parked my car outside, and the date was going really badly, but we were only half way through the food. I panicked, looked out the window and shouted: 'Oh my god, someone's hit my car!' (I was already missing a wing mirror.) I shot out of the restaurant (the owner knew me, and I could have paid him later), but when I ran, the lady ran with me, and chased me down the street! I got in my car and drove after him, thinking I had made good my escape. The woman was so worried, she called the police, and I ended up filing a completely made-up story, so as not to waste their time! I wish I had just come clean! **❞**

Matt, Love and Friends

Date expectations

Most people find the first moments of a 'blind date' nerve-wracking. You may have spoken for months, formed all kinds of ideas in your head of the person, but you still don't really know them. It's even hard to know how to say hello – a handshake seems too formal, a kiss on the cheek too forward.

How do you greet your internet date?

Simple hello – 31 per cent
Shake hands – 14 per cent
Kiss on cheek – 55 per cent
(*Love @ First Site* survey on Date the UK)

This meeting with your familiar stranger is a moment of truth, as Susan from Soulmates points out. 'You always feel really vulnerable because in that moment you're being judged on what you look like. I often find myself wishing I'd used a less flattering picture, or written "could lose a few pounds" rather than "slim".'

It's hard not to let your true feelings show, especially if you're less than impressed. 'One time I was so shocked by the difference between photograph and reality that my jaw nearly hit the floor. Trying to put my features back into neutral almost killed me', says Tim from Jdate.

Ricky Gervais' David Brent character summed up perfectly the disappointment you can feel in the 2003 *Office* Christmas special. His reaction on seeing his date: 'Oh, for f***'s sake.'

Instant reaction

Never has the maxim that you only get one chance to make a

first impression been truer than in internet dating. In some cases it's a matter of minutes. Our survey revealed that 15 per cent of people make up their mind within the first five minutes while 25 per cent will give you half an hour. Richard from Love and Friends observes: 'Opinions are often reached on first sight, and seldom change after that.'

But giving so little time to people can be counterproductive. 'It's like when you first start a new job and the new person you thought was not particularly pretty, handsome or even interesting gradually seems very attractive', says Ko from Love and Friends.

Fortunately nearly half wait to the end of a date to decide if a person is a potential match, and a third will go on a second date to be sure. As Bickle from Soulmates points out, the immediacy of internet dating can engender a 'grass is always greener' approach. 'Some people treat internet dates like buses – you don't have to jump on board, because another one will be along in a minute. But if someone makes the effort to meet, you should at least try and get to know them.'

First date disasters

❝I went round to a woman's house on a first date, she sounded very friendly, but when I got there she wanted me to do some DIY.**❞**

Julian, Match

❝I met this bloke and all was going OK until he got a phone call. It was his mum wanting to know how the date was going, what I was like, and what he wanted for dinner. Apparently his mum always took a keen interest in his dates.**❞**

Caite, Love and Friends

"As soon as we met, my date wanted to know my date of birth. I thought she wanted to check if I had lied about my age. Then she asked for my time of birth. She was doing this numerology on me to see if we were compatible, and told me she would have to leave if the numbers didn't add up. I left instead. **"**

Travis, Soulmates

"I had to drive my date to a party and we were following her mates who knew the way. But after 30 minutes I realised I'd been following the wrong car. We still talk, but the romance died that evening. **"**

Kerr, Love and Friends

"I once met two Bens in one week. The first was lovely, the second absolutely awful. Of course the inevitable happened – the nice one texted me to ask me how my other date had gone and I replied to the wrong Ben. The first I knew of it? When Ben no. 2 texted me and said: 'Glad you think I'm a total twat!' **"**

Jane, Soulmates

"After arranging to meet online, this guy decided to bring four male friends with him. At first I couldn't work out which one was my online date, and then it seemed that it was some kind of lottery. Whoever fancied me would give the nod, and the others would make excuses and leave. I saved them the bother by making a hasty exit. **"**

Janet, Udate

"We met at a pizza place, ordered two pizzas and a bottle of wine and I went to the loo. When I came back she was legging it out of the restaurant with her coat flying behind her. She saw me returning and yelled across the room, 'That's my bus!' I'm not sure what was more embarrassing, her clearly not fancying me and doing a runner, or trying to explain things to the waiter. **"**

Richard, Love and Friends

"We had spoken for a few weeks, no pictures had been exchanged, but we got on really well. We were around the same age (or so I thought) and we decided to meet at her local. I went to the pub to find this woman who was nothing like her description. She burst out crying and confessed that she was 35 and married. She wasn't getting any sex from hubby and wanted to meet someone from the internet for a shag. My excuses were made and I left. **"**

Kevin, Soulmates

"I had a long, sexy phone build-up to a date. But when we met it turned out to be turgidly flat – with none of the buzz and sparkle. After a while I got suspicious, and she eventually confessed that she was my original date's friend who had come in her place. Apparently the original woman had found someone, and sent her mate because she was single. **"**

Kevin, Udate

"This date got us tickets for Hamlet. I knew I was in trouble when the lights went down and he pulled out the text of the play and started making notes in the margin. In the interval, he turned to me, and asked, 'Have you ever been out with a genius before?' Once I'd stopped laughing, he looked really hurt and said that he was serious. He was really peeved when I made it clear he was not coming back with me. The next day, I sent a thank you text and said 'next time it's on me'. His reply was: 'No, next time it's in you.' What a cheek! **"**

Sarah, Udate

"I met a date for coffee, and half way through the evening he took off his shoes and socks and proceeded to massage his feet. Funnily enough, there was no second date. **"**

Helen, Love and Friends

Parting shots

One of the most difficult moments of a first date is saying goodbye. What is the other person thinking? What if they like you, and you don't like them? What if you like them, and they don't like you? What if you like them, but don't know if they like you?

The art of parting with your dignity intact and still leaving a hint of your intentions is a subtle, but important, one. Whatever you say at the end of the date will be read as a coded message (even if it is not).

'I'm a bit of a chicken. I usually say I'll ring them and then don't', says Jane from Match. 'This is purely because I'm female and worry that some men might get aggressive about being rejected.' Brian from Love and Friends says: 'I suggest a "review" towards the end of the night. If they say they don't like me then I can safely say the same to them.'

One of the tricks is to have an open-ended remark to hand, for example, 'Thanks for coming, it's been good to meet you, let's keep in touch.'

A well-rehearsed parting line is handy, but some people are left floundering, not knowing whether to shake hands or give a quick peck on the cheek. The latter, if unreciprocated, can leave you puckering into thin air – never a good look for anyone.

The peck on the cheek, of course, can be misinterpreted, as Carole from Udate says: 'You don't know if someone is going for a full-blown snog, which some men seem to think is par for the course.' The important thing is to read the signals. If the lady in question is halfway down the street shouting 'I'll email you', her scarf pulled up to her nose, it's not generally an invitation to follow.

Do you tell people if you want to see them again at the end of a date?

Yes: 43 per cent
No: 57 per cent
Love @ First Site survey on Date the UK

One of the advantages of internet dating is using an email to test the water the next day. You can tell someone you don't feel a spark, or encourage them if you want to take the relationship further. Nobody likes to be rejected, but a friendly, clear email is perhaps the easiest way to let people know what you think.

There will always be a few people who won't take no for an answer.

'Dating'

The majority of online daters are looking for a serious relationship – our survey showed that fewer than one in twenty date more than one person at a time (and the content of their profiles usually distinguishes them). But in the pheromonal excitement of internet dating, it's easy for wires to get crossed. Profiles say 'I am looking for love' – but few add that they intend to enjoy the search.

So, once you start seeing someone, how do you know if he or she has called off the search or is still trying to find the prize? 'You can often tell what people really think about you by going online', says Mary from Love and Friends. 'Check the last date they logged on. If they are still poking around the site when you've met them a few times, then you might need to find out how serious they are.'

And when someone does remove their profile from a site, 'it's a symbolic "lowering of the flag"', says Susan from Soulmates. 'It means I am no longer on the market.' When should you do this? There's no rule, but Jane from Match says: 'When do I take my profile down? When I've shagged them.'

And if you continue to log on, think about the signals you are sending out to them. 'Does it mean you are keeping it light, still looking around?', asks Mary. 'Will they think you are not interested, or that you are stalking them? The way it is set up means you can easily become a cyber spy.'

And the transparency of internet dating means that people can be caught out.

❝❝I started seeing a guy from a site. But I felt a bit unsure about him, so after a couple of weeks I logged on under a different name and sure enough he was still a regular visitor. What was worse was that he emailed my new profile, and told me he was single. So I told him a little about my imaginary self and he suggested we meet for a date. In *real life* we were already due to meet that Friday, so I suggested Friday, and sure enough he blew me out. Said an old friend of his was coming down from Scotland. And no, I did not turn up to give him a shock. But he rang about 9 on Friday and left a message to say his friend had missed the train, and was I still free!!! I did not bother returning his call, or any other calls after that!**❞❞**

Shelly, Match

Long distance dating

Most of the big dating sites were born in the US. Udate, Match and Friendfinder all began stateside, and then added other countries. So it's not surprising that occasionally you will get an email from someone who lives beyond our shores.

Internet dating with someone who lives in another country has a mysterious appeal. But unlike holiday romances – where you meet the person first – the logistics of getting together with an American, for example, are tricky. There is a lot more at stake if somebody goes all the way to New York for a blind date. You can't just leave them after half an hour.

Liz met Paolo from New York on Match.com:

" Before flying out to meet Paolo, I had plans in hand should things not have been right for either of us. Guess we were lucky. In the end the difficulty was not going for a date with a man who lived in NY, which was a fun thing to do, but the unexpectedness of actually falling in love and then having to deal with the painful reality of us being in two different countries without the immediate possibility of either moving to where the other was. Distance can intensify emotions, longing, etc.; the relationship is often based on a few action-packed days together every now and then rather than a slow burning, once or twice a week meet up. He ended up with huge phone bills, and in the early days we were on the phone every day for up to five hours a day – sometimes all night long. Distance is definitely something to consider if you are going to date someone who lives 100 miles away, let alone 1,000 or even more. Even though in the end it couldn't work out, we have remained the best of friends and – two years on – we still talk from time to time. **"**

Enjoy yourself

Some people treat internet dates like job interviews: they line up five or six dates a week or, in some cases, several dates in one day. One lady we know gave each of her dates half-hour slots, and simply moved between two different bars to make sure they didn't bump into each other.

You've got to kiss a lot of frogs to find a prince/princess. And at times frog-kissing can be a frustrating experience. Internet dating should be fun. We have heard from hundreds of people whose lives have been enriched by dating – and if you try not to take it too seriously, yours will be too.

— Chapter 8 —

INSIGHTS ON OUT-SITES

Gay Dating

What you want when you want it

If internet dating has shaken up the straight dating world it has turned the male gay scene upside down. So much so that, as one person put it, 'if you're *not* internet dating, people think something's wrong with you'.

One megasite – Gaydar – dominates. Membership is almost equivalent to a 'gay passport'. As one Gaydar member says, 'People don't swap phone numbers any more, they exchange Gaydar profiles.'

Gaydar is so embedded in gay culture that if you talk about meeting someone in the 'Bloke shop', on 'The Line' or on Blowmenow.com, everybody knows you mean Gaydar. Visit a bar in Manchester's Canal Street or Old Compton Street in Soho, and it will be only a matter of time before you hear the 'G' word. Dave, who met his partner on Gaydar, says, 'You're sitting outside a café and someone will remark: "There's Newboi21. It's been a while since he was 21, let me tell you!"'

The site had humble beginnings – created in 1999 by a South African couple in London who wanted to find a date for a single friend. Since then, worldwide membership has trebled every year. By the end of 1999 it had 60,000 members; at the start of 2005 membership had reached almost 2.5 million. Of those, 800,000 are in the UK – one in every 50 Britons.

Site veterans claim Gaydar has changed dramatically in its short life, contending that its growth has been matched by an increase in sexual content. And, for all Gaydar's protestations, its tagline – 'What you want when you want it' – tends to confirm this argument.

The proliferation of nude profile pictures compels others to join in.

> *I vowed never to take my clothes off but peer pressure has changed all that. Now I have a picture of me in my Speedos, shot at a jaunty angle.*
>
> Ben

Jamie Crick – head of Gaydar PR – rejects the sex-only tag, maintaining that Gaydar is an 'online community driven by members' needs. When you log on you can choose to indicate if you're "looking for a relationship", or want to "hook up now" – it's up to you. We've designed the site to reflect what gay people want – whether that is a relationship or sex.' He sees the site as a virtual bar: 'There will be some men looking to pick up, some looking for love. But I have yet to meet a gay man who doesn't want to meet the love of his life.'

It's true you can avoid the sexual content, as each Gaydar profile is classified with a coloured dot: red (explicit sexual content), yellow (some nudity), or blue (no sexual content). So if you're simply after friends to chat with, you can side-step the 'cock shots' and stick to blue dotted profiles.

Crick points out that the site appears red dot heavy because 'the red dots linger for longer. These members are addicts who are permanently online, while the blue dots tend to visit once or twice a week to check emails and message people.'

But, for all Gaydar's 'community' claims, it's become the gay equivalent of a 'take-away'. Thanks to the 'Gaydar Positioning System', you can now get a man round in the time it takes to order a pizza. Just key in your postcode and Bob's your uncle – or your next shag at least.

Gaydar caters for every permutation under the sun. Search menus are long and varied. If your dream man is a Catalan-speaking, ice-skating 'bear' (think beardy type like Bjorn in Abba) with a fetish for 'fur' and 'frottage', then the keyword search will take you to him. Alternatively, if brains are your bag, you can search out a word like 'eclectic' to sort the men from the boys – a trick employed by one member who says 'size matters – but only in terms of IQ'.

The site's 'transparency' makes it a stalker's paradise. When someone's online you can see their exact whereabouts on the site – you can also see if they want a 'boyfriend', a 'date', to 'hook up now', or 'hook up later'. A profile-tracking device lets you earmark 'hotties' so you – or they – can make contact later. Alternatively, you can cover your tracks and cruise from behind a virtual bush.

Hitwise – an internet company which measures the number of hits a site gets – says people logging on to Gaydar spend an average of 30 minutes online. This is hardly surprising given that, as one member puts it, 'the site has enough gizmos to make your eyes glaze over'.

So what influence has Gaydar – and internet dating in general – had on male gay culture?

Only gay in the village

For urban gay men online dating is just another 'weapon' (no giggling at the back) in the cruising armoury, but for those elsewhere – in particular younger men who have yet to come out – it has had a deeper social impact.

As internet dater Clive says: 'Dafydd-off-*Little-Britain* types suddenly realise they're not "the only gay in the village" and can have contact with the outside world.' Andrew agrees: 'Until I was 18, I lived in a small town in Wales. I had no idea how many gay men there were nearby until I joined Gaydar! To say it changed my life would be putting it mildly!'

Online dating has also dispensed with the need for cottaging. Although, as Ben points out, 'there will always be men who are into voyeurism and who like the feel of bark on skin!'

Scene queen

For those who don't have access to 'the scene' or baulk at squeezing into a tight white T-shirt, dating sites are a godsend. Paul from OUTeverywhere says: 'The internet has created an alternative virtual "community" that exists in parallel to Soho or Canal Street. And for some users it does away with the need for those places at all.' Gary agrees: 'Online dating is a boon for those who are not Danni Minogue fans. Now non-scene types who don't want to chat up men in bars can stay in on the pull, actively or passively.'

Passive pulling is possible on Gaydar thanks to its instant messaging system. Users can simply log on in the morning and remain logged on all day, responding only when the 'Gaydar Assistant' informs them someone's said hello.

'This means you are always available, even if you're doing the washing up', says Chris, a long-standing Gaydar member. 'I call it "leaving out the crab pot" – if anybody "bites", you hear a beep and you can respond immediately.'

The Gaydar messaging system is a very popular facet of the site. Many members – including those who have found a boyfriend on the site – carry on using it to talk to friends. Simon's profile, for example, specifically states that he has a boyfriend, but has chosen to keep his profile live so that he can stay in contact with his Gaydar friends. 'I love it because I can also talk to people from back home in the States', he says.

Size matters

Love or loathe it, Gaydar's size guarantees it a certain success. Most of the men we talked to said they use other sites but still keep their profile on Gaydar.

The vast choice keeps daters like Steve coming back for more: 'Because it's so big, you can turn it into whatever you want.' And Paul – who is only interested in long-term relationships – says he's spoken to people he would never have met offline: 'I have had many meaningful interactions with people from all over the world.' He disputes the claim that Gaydar is merely a 'sex super-market'. 'The fascinating thing about Gaydar is that it is this amorphous creature that can be turned into an ugly or pretty thing, it's up to you.'

Getting the habit

But Gaydar's superior size and instant access to potential dates has a downside – the temptation not to 'let go'. Some members confess to being slightly – or in some cases completely – addicted to Gaydar.

❝It holds out a nebulous, perpetual possibility – you never know when the next great guy will come along. It's like gambling in Vegas, you keep pulling those handles. **❞**

Chris

> **❝** *The first thing I do when I get up in the morning is switch on the computer, have a fag and go to 'New Members'.* **❞**

Steve

And some say while they don't like the way the site has changed over the years, they can't keep away. 'It's like New Labour – when it first started, everyone was very excited about it, now we feel betrayed by it, let down. Yet we stick with it because there's no real alternative.'

Internet dating has entranced the male gay world. If you want proof of this, visit any central London internet café at weekends. Paul, a Glaswegian, was amazed when he first arrived in London three years ago:

> **❝** *After the clubs had closed, my flatmate dragged me into an internet café in the wee hours of a Saturday morning. The Charing Cross Road branch of Easyeverything was teeming with gay men trawling Gaydar chatrooms. There was this 'meerkat' effect as people popped up from behind their computers to locate the person in the café they were talking to online. Sadly my flatmate didn't get lucky – his desperate need to 'pull' took on tragic proportions as the last of the crowd paired up and trickled out through the bright orange doors.* **❞**

Life beyond Gaydar

So Gaydar seems to have got the pink online market sewn up – or has it?

Already a number of sites have sprung up which offer an alternative to the 'full-on, blow me now experience', as one dater put it. OUTeverywhere (formerly OUT in the UK) – with its distinct home-from-home appeal – is the main contender in

Britain. Its stated 'USP' is to 'give every gay person an open and safe environment in which to interact without prejudice or exploitation and without an emphasis on sex'.

'Post an even slightly racy photograph on OUT and you'll be thrown off', warns Ben – a member of both Gaydar and OUT. He claims that OUT's numbers have picked up significantly in recent months thanks to an influx of 'disillusioned Gaydar members'.

OUT's emphasis on 'community' clearly wins over many daters. Colin, another user of both Gaydar and OUT, says if he gets a green tick of approval from someone on OUT he's more likely to respond. Why? 'Because on OUT they're more likely to be genuinely interested whereas a Gaydar guy might just be "online, hot and horny".'

Jaketm.org, meanwhile, is in a league of its own. It calls itself a 'professional, networking community', although others, albeit cynical others, call it 'middle-class Gaydar'. Rob pinpoints the key difference. 'On Gaydar in the job section, most people put, "Who cares? Does it matter?" On Jake you get a full CV including the number of A's at O Level.'

Andrew met his boyfriend on Jake and still uses the site to chat to friends. He points out that Jake members illustrate the 'schizophrenic nature' of gay dating. 'Jake is supposed to be professional with lots of men in suits but then sometimes you see the same men on Gaydar … in a harness!'

The main advantages of Jake, says one member, 'are the organised events which are really good especially if you're new to London and you want to meet a certain class of gay man'. But, he says, 'you have to have a high tolerance for name-droppers – people going on about who did what to whom last night at the Sanderson or while skiing at the weekend.'

Jake's business-like façade makes it office-friendly. David says: 'It has none of the porny pop-ups you get on other sites, so you can log on at work, safe in the knowledge nothing "gay" will go through your work server.'

Same old, same old

Of course, gay sites are no different from straight sites when it comes to profiles. There is the same scope for self-delusion, the same little 'white lies' – the same recipes for disaster.

William, an OUTeverywhere member, says: 'One of internet

Success stories

There are also success stories. Anthony met his current boy-friend on Gaydar after eighteen months of 'fun'.

❝*I don't believe in love at first sight. But I do believe in empathy. When I saw him I knew we'd get on well. Ten hours later we were kissing and holding hands. The following week I told him I was changing my profile from 'looking for a relationship' to 'friends'. Two days after that we both agreed to delete our profiles altogether and we've been together ever since.* ❞

Steve met Olly on Jake:

❝*I ignored him at first because he sounded a bit pretentious – 'loft in Bow, commercials director, novel on the way' – but then we talked on the phone and got on really well. On our first date I was so blown away by his beauty when he walked in that my first instinct was to hide behind my menu. I then proceeded to get hideously, embarrassingly drunk, so much so that he had to escort me home. And that was it – the rest, as they say, is history. He never left really!* ❞

dating's biggest pros is also, paradoxically, its biggest con. It allows people to establish an identity for themselves which leaves reality behind as it turns all "Madame Bovary". The reality of meeting in real life often falls short of the online experience.'

Harry from Gaydar agrees: 'My first "date" was with a guy called "Italian Puro" (his real name was Federico – but curiously I always think of him by his online name). His photo showed a lean, handsome Italian guy in his late teens. In reality, there had been many a lasagne for Italian Puro since the photograph was taken, and he tasted of Lambert and Butler cigarettes.'

The sites

www.gay.com

They say: 'Premium personals, chat, engaging content, shopping guides and community services have made Gay.com one of the largest gay online communities in the world.'

We say: With several million members, and offshoot sites in several countries, gay.com is not so much a dating site as an online network offering information on HIV, religion, coming out, and films. Members are from across the spectrum so there is something for everyone. Gay.com's empire takes in Australia (au.gay.com) and Latin America (latino.gay.com) as well as much of Europe. The downside of the UK site is its all-American feel, replete with warnings about vulgarity and discussions on the struggle to be gay and Christian. That said, the java chat rooms are sometimes downright filthy. Few people use gay.com for finding relationships, and most access it for the immediate gratification of chat, be it cybersex or 'the real deal'.

Usability: The profiles are easy to browse and free to respond to. The message boards give users the opportunity to express their views on gay life and possibly meet someone in the process.

Cost: Basic membership is free but a Premium Personals and Chat Subscription costs $42.95 for three months; a week's trial membership will set you back $9.95.

Membership: 3.5 million worldwide. Also has lesbian members.

www.gaydarguys.co.uk

They say: 'Simply the biggest gay dating website in the world!'

We say: That's a bit of an exaggeration, but it's certainly the biggest in the UK. One look at the pictures shows that Gaydar embraces the wishes of all gay men, from the chino-clad boy-next-door to the gimp in the leather mask. By far the most impressive feature of Gaydar is the searches. The GPS (Gaydar Positioning System) locates people with the same postcode, thus shedding a new light on home delivery. The site even has its own radio station to entertain you while you surf. The average age is 25–35.

Usability: Gaydar has attempted to simplify the mind-boggling number of ways you can find other people. Advanced users can search by location, keywords in profiles or hair colour, and be informed when people register who fit the bill. The profiles are censor-free, except, of course, if you include a picture of yourself as a child.

Cost: Free as long as you're happy with a limited number of messages and only basic search abilities. A modest £9 a month bags you unlimited messages and full search abilities.

Membership: UK: 800,000, Australia: 190,000, New Zealand: 11,000, Worldwide: 2.4 million

www.jaketm.org

They say: Re-launched in late 2001, this 'online social, professional, networking community' was founded and sponsored by independent financial advisors Ivan Massow.

We say: It likes to think it's a networking community for professional gay men, but many use it for dating. If you can stand the techno-babble, including potential dates being referred to as the 'community' or the 'population', then Jake makes a refreshing change to sites which add a new meaning to the phrase 'all talk and no trousers'. It appeals to the professional upwardly mobile gay man who thinks he's above Gaydar. An interesting touch is the 'Edit prod' feature where you can input four questions you would like 'the community' to respond to, for example 'click here if you would like a beer', 'click here if you think we should work together'.

Usability: Pretty smooth although the split window set-up can be a bit irritating after a while.

Cost: A tenner a month will get you access to events and 'business briefings', and 'a nice shiny Jake membership card'. A free 30-day trial membership allows you to test the water.

Membership: 19,000 worldwide, but most members are based in London.

www.outeverywhere.com

They say: Relaunched in 2005 after ten years as OUT in the UK, the site promises 'zero exploitation of gay people'.

We say: Despite the 'we-mean-business' makeover, and new fee structure, the site's values (see above) remain the same. However, as the name change suggests, the site's focus is now more than ever on group activities for members to meet in the 'real world'. There is a heavy bias against the traditional 'scene' of clubbing and cruising, and this comes across in an almost pious manner throughout the site. Members may appear to be nice boys – but how many are wearing leather beneath that cardie?

Usability: The new-look OUT, with its cleaner, more streamlined design, makes a refreshing change from its headache-inducing, split-screen predecessor. Its pally, inclusive style (you get a message from the boss when you join) is very appealing – especially for jaded Gaydar folk.

Cost: £5 a month with discounts for students and the unemployed

Membership: 30,000 members worldwide, but most are UK-based. Has around 3,000 lesbian members.

The L word

So what effect has internet dating had on lesbian life? The Sapphic world is a compact universe. As one woman puts it: 'There are only so many ladies to go around. And it gets a bit claustrophobic when every lesbian you know has slept with all your friends.'

So online dating has allowed many lesbians to graze in pastures new. What's more, they can do this away from the disapproving gaze of a public who still haven't quite come to terms with the concept of lesbian love.

As Liz James, founder of The Pink Sofa, puts it: 'For many lesbians – whether they are coming out, in the closet, sick of clubs, or simply in search of a much wider choice – the internet is the best thing since sliced bread. It's a convenient, private and non-judgmental way to find a partner.'

It's also a way of avoiding the 'scene', which for many women is quite alienating. As Sarah says, 'Many women feel the scene doesn't represent them and creates an unbalanced view of what a lesbian actually is.' Others think it's too daunting. Karen from Gaydar Girls says: 'Unless you're a scene queen or great with chat-up lines, it can be hard to meet new people – online dating has changed that.'

But love and relationships are not the be all and end all of lesbian online life. On many sites the emphasis is less on dating and more on friendship and support – offering a lifeline for those in the process of coming out.

Dating was the last thing on Jacky's mind when she first logged on: 'It was a source of support and knowledge, to be able to read other women's experiences, and ask their advice – I never thought of finding partners there.'

Badgirls

Some lesbian sites have emerged in mysterious ways. Badgirls-online started as an e-zine homage to the ITV prison drama Bad Girls. In its heyday it had 80,000 hits a month. But in the midst of discussions on the message boards about who did what to whom and why, some women were experiencing dramas of their own. 'I suddenly realised what I'd been missing', says Stacey, who was married at the time. 'I know it's corny but it was like coming home!'

The site's founder, Sally Blackmore, says many would-be lesbians were encouraged by the 'normality' of the lesbian characters. 'For the first time on TV there were two normal-looking, pretty women falling in love. This encouraged many women to come out; we still get emails from people saying: "Without Bad Girls we wouldn't have met – this site changed my life."'

Sally and her partner have gone on to set up a dating site

which offers an alternative to 'Gaydar Girls and some of the seedier sites'. Girl Meets Girl – which started in February 2004 – is open to everybody – 'straights' and 'not sures' included. The number of members without profiles (3,000) compared to the number of members with profiles (850) suggests the open approach is working, appealing to many who are 'just looking' and want to test the water.

Gaydar Girls

Gaydar Girls is the most popular lesbian and bisexual site. Its size means it can satisfy a wide variety of requirements – from friendship and relationships, to easily accessible sex.

As Liz says, 'Gaydar can be whatever you want it to be. Sometimes you just want to browse, sometimes you want a date for the weekend, and sometimes you just want to chat to your mates.'

In big cities it provides a direct link to the lesbian scene.

❝ *Gaydar Girls gives you a sense of community. It's like home. Everyone I meet on the London scene seems to be on there. It also works the other way round: you can meet people in bars and then look up their profiles online.* **❞**

Karen

❝ *If you see someone you like in a club but don't get to talk to them – you can find them on the site on Monday morning and strike up a conversation.* **❞**

Liz, Brighton

What's not to like?

As on any site there are 'appealing' and 'less appealing' profiles. The worst offenders include:

- Profiles with pictures of cats ('These are alarming: what are you going to do – send your cat on a date?')
- Nudity ('Why would you?')
- Women that camp out online 24/7 thanks to broadband (These are the ones that use an 'out of office' reply like 'back soon' when they go out – best to avoid these as there's a faint whiff of desperation to them.)
- People who say 'Shy at first but a nutter when you get to know me' ('I can't wait.')
- People who write about their exes (These are definite no-nos – it's so obvious they've just split up.)
- Profiles that say 'I don't like liars or cheats' (This usually says more about the person writing the profile than anything else.)
- People who say 'No butches' (Translation: 'I'm not completely out yet' or 'I don't want to be seen as a lesbian and get shouted at in the street.')
- Profiles that say nothing at all ('These are most likely to be straight women wanting to experiment or dodgy men.')
- Profiles that say 'No baggage!' ('Who, over a certain age, is really baggage-free?')
- Those that attempt to ape the casual, up-for-it elements of Gaydar 'proper' ('Sad.')

Catherine, a long-standing Gaydar member, says a lot of women post profiles which read like a lesbian handbook. 'I have lost count of the number of people who claim that *The L Word* [American cult TV series] is their favourite TV programme or who put "something by Sarah Waters" under "favourite book". Some really go to town on how much of a cool-daddy, scene puppy they are in the "fave clubs" section. Some even put clubs in San Francisco or Madrid – when they just walked past them on holiday!'

'And a lot of women', she points out, 'won't tick the "shag" box even when that's what they're after. Probably because being forward makes people think one is mad, male or a couple looking for a threesome.'

'Another frustration on Gaydar is the tendency to "dumb down". I was attracted to one woman's profile because she said she liked intellectual debate. When I asked her what she meant by intellectual, she said, "No cybersex!"'

Non-lesbian sites

So what about the mainstream sites? Why do some women prefer these?

Quite simply, says Soulmates member 'Elastigirl', because lesbians are not defined only by their sexuality. 'I'm first and foremost a *Guardian* reader rather than a lesbian.'

Another woman says she chose a mixed site – Love and Friends – because she was sick of the labels and categories that plague gay sites. 'The "No butches/No bi's" attitude that you get on some profiles gets really tiresome. I don't consider myself to be butch, femme, or anything, just me.'

But an obvious drawback on non-specific sites is numbers. 'I spent about an hour and a half filling out all the questionnaires on Ivory Towers, only to find there were only five other lesbians on there!' says Irene. 'Fortunately they were kind enough to refund my subscription.'

Then there are 'technical' problems, which can lead to misunderstandings. 'Sometimes when I search for matches I am offered straight women or even men in the results, presumably because they've accidentally ticked the wrong box at some point during the registration procedure', says Vicky.

So what are the downsides to online dating?

Men

Men posing as women to live out their fantasy of girl-on-girl action are a constant irritation on lesbian sites – both for those who use them and for those who run them. Liz James says: 'Although The Pink Sofa's subscription fee acts as a deterrent, a few men still manage to slip through the net. But our members "dob" them in, and they are removed immediately.'

Some men are better at disguising themselves than others. Gaydar Girls member Clare says she and her girlfriend used to play 'spot the bloke'. 'We got to the point where we could tell a male "infiltrator" just from the way they composed their mail – men tend to use capitals and lots of LOL.' Others are less subtle. 'They start off all nice and friendly, then you comment on the weather and they respond with "I want to lick your pussy"!' says Julie, another Gaydar Girls member. The best way to sort them out? 'Just mention periods', says Jane. 'That normally gets rid of them.'

Such complaints are not directed solely at men. Some lesbians mistrust bisexual women in the belief they are foils for male partners. Angela says: 'There are a lot of couples looking for a girl to have a threesome with, which is unnerving because they always seem to contact me!'

And Sally, from The Pink Sofa, has become wary of bisexual women after a couple of bad experiences. 'I'd been chatting for a couple of weeks to a girl I really liked. She insisted that I go round for dinner. When I walked in, the first thing she said was: "Sally, meet Matt."'

Too much too soon

The excitement at finding a kindred spirit in a relatively small 'pool' can lead to a scenario summed up by the joke: 'What does a lesbian take on her second date? A removal van!' Stereotypical though this may be, it's an experience shared by many online daters:

> *I met this woman who was very, very nice and we got on really well. But then, on the second date, she suggested we lived together. Needless to say, I didn't contact her again.*
>
> Karen, Gaydar Girls

> *One woman asked me to meet her after we'd exchanged a couple of sentences. When I gently suggested she might want to slow down, she got very cross and presumed I was playing with her feelings.*
>
> Sarah, The Pink Sofa

> *I met this girl from Gaydar a few times and thought, yes, she seems lovely. Until she called me at three in the morning with the news that she'd booked us an appointment at a fertility clinic so we could get some sperm.*
>
> Alison, Gaydar Girls

Mirror, mirror

Naturally, online dating has the same drawbacks for the lesbian community as it does for everybody else. 'There is a tendency for online dating to be almost whimsical and 2D. It doesn't really become reality until you both meet up and then there is a real chance that your bubble will burst', says Angela from Gaydar Girls.

Whether bubbles burst more often in the lesbian community is debatable. There is the same tendency for self-aggrandisement – 'women who say they're creative but really work in admin and make candles in their spare time' – and the same potential for self-delusion – 'I had a date once with a girl who'd said she was very feminine and looked like Catherine Zeta-Jones. When she turned up, she looked more like Phil Mitchell.'

But for many lesbians, and would-be lesbians, internet dating has opened up a whole new world of opportunity, allowing them to make friends, find lovers and access support networks which can sometimes be lacking offline.

Brief (and not so brief) encounters

"I was completely besotted by this woman, I would race home every night to log on in the hope of catching her online. So I was extremely excited by the prospect of meeting her. In my mind I had built a whole profile about her far beyond the profile she had on the internet. But the evening I met her was one of the worst nights of my life. We had nothing to say to each other: she was not my type, not on my wavelength and my physical image of her was at odds with the reality. Luckily I had met my now-girlfriend the night before! **"**

Cath, Gaydar Girls

"I met my last partner online three years ago. We got chatting over concert tickets and in true lesbian style we met two weeks later and fell in love. Sadly after two years she met someone else off the same site and I was history. Not that I'm bitter or anything! **"**

Helen, Gingerbeer

> **❝**Gaydar was a breakthrough for me. I started off my Gaydar life in Brighton and wanted to move to London, but was scared because I didn't know anyone there. I got chatting to a few people, grew my confidence and moved up the next month. **❞**
>
> Bella, Gaydar Girls

> **❝**I was contacted by a white witch from Wales, several people old enough to be my mother and numerous women who were after a dodgy threesome. I've accidentally displayed a photo of a very large-breasted woman on my computer screen in a busy internet café and on another occasion cottoned on too late that Dominatrice wasn't chosen because it was a pretty name. **❞**
>
> Sarah, Gaydar Girls

> **❝**I remember receiving four or five emails – each of which I deleted for one reason or another (too sexual, too bland, etc.) but this one just jumped out of the screen at me – it was brief, friendly and interesting. Over the next few days we emailed one another – I think Alison still has the emails and it's amazing to look back on them now, at the absolute intensity and suddenness of it all. It was definitely love at first screen. The funny thing is, knowing her as I do now, she hardly uses the computer – she had literally stumbled across the site as well and had never posted or replied to any adverts on such sites before. **❞**
>
> Karen, Gaydar Girls

The sites

www.gaydargirls.com

They say: 'Gaydar Girls has grown rapidly since its launch in 2002 and is due for a redesign in 2005.'

We say: Unlike its big brother, the female arm (or should that be rib?) of Gaydar is totally free. That means you can email and send instant messages to people, search for who's online (according to geographical location) and use the chat rooms to your heart's content. Many members stay logged in all day, leaving 'out of office'-style markers when they leave their desks so as not to miss a trick. And while some consider the site to have more 'Muffulikes' than 'Sapphicsisters', its size means you can easily find friends and meet potential partners. There are some nude pictures (a few clearly inspired by *It Should Never Happen to a Vet*) but, as on Gaydar Guys, you can side-step these thanks to the rating system of coloured dots.

Usability: The message archiving system is unnecessarily complicated but once you get into the habit of saving every message, you'll be fine.

Cost: Free

Membership: UK: 80,000, Australia: 10,000, New Zealand: 335

www.gingerbeer.co.uk

They say: Gingerbeer (cockney rhyming slang for queer) is 'the most comprehensive guide to London's Lesbian scene'. Now in its fifth year, it provides information on lesbian venues and club nights; it also details support groups, sporting activities and entertainment listings.

We say: Run entirely by volunteers, Gingerbeer is more of an 'online community' than a dating site. Members can meet each other at organised events or via the thriving – and very varied – message boards. These include the 'Creative Writing Lab', the 'Purr Love Lounge', and the 'Dungeon' for those who want to discuss their 'darker passions'. The site's cheeky 'Lesbefriends' section gives you the chance to 'put your school on the lesbian map'. There's even a Lesbeforum where you can quiz old school chums and find out whether Hayley the head girl really did bat for the other side.

Usability: Well-run, good-looking and very user-friendly

Cost: Free

UK membership: 6,000 visitors to site every week

www.girlmeetsgirl.co.uk

They say: Friendly interactive place for women to meet other women.

We say: This fledgling site was set up in 2004 to cater for those who may be put off by the 'in-your-face' quality of some lesbian sites. The softly-softly approach is evident from the minute you hit the home page – never mind the L word, it doesn't even mention the W word!

Usability: Attractive modern graphics in tasteful burgundy make the site a pleasure to use. The 'neeeeed beer' and 'hello pumpkin' postcards are a nice touch.

Cost: Full membership costs £5 per month

UK membership: 800 profiles, but 3,000 active users

www.thepinksofa.co.uk

They say: Based in New Zealand, The Pink Sofa is the most popular online lesbian dating site in the world. It's a friendly, comfortable meeting place for lesbians and bi-females, genuinely wanting to meet others, which does not tolerate sleaze or curiosity.

We say: This is a friendly, informal and well-run site. The subscription fee means women are more likely to mean business than on a free site. Nice that it sticks to its policy of only allowing people to post pictures of themselves – and not their pets! Members can use a variety of features to contact and get to know other members – they can mail each other, chat in the public chat rooms, use the site's instant messenger system or get a sense of someone from their posts on the public forums/message boards.

Usability: Slick and easy to use

Cost: £10 for one month, £20 for three months. On registration, you automatically get a three-day free trial of premier membership

Membership: UK: 7,500, Australia and New Zealand: 15,000

Chapter 9

ON THE CYBERCOUCH

An Expert Guide to Online Dating

It takes nerve to put yourself in love's internet shop-window. Even the most level-headed person won't cross the dating battlefield without some minor injuries.

There is always a sense of rejection when you don't get a response to your mail: you thought you were a 9, suddenly you feel like a 6; you realise that without the face-to-face banter to get you into the ladies' good books virtual flirting leaves you floundering.

On the other hand, a never-ending stream of mail may create the sensation that you are a cyberspace love-god. The whole dating world is clamouring for you, the only problem is that now you have to meet people in the real world.

Whichever way cupid's arrow falls, you're on show. So how can we prepare ourselves? We brought together three relationship experts, and asked them for a strategy to navigate the choppy seas of cyber romance.

Jamie Smart is an NLP (Neuro-Linguistic Programming) trainer, and an expert on communication and change.

Sarah Whittaker is a holistic therapist and homeopath, specialising in emotional problems and personal development.

Max Blumberg is a relationship psychologist and psychotherapist, who has appeared on a variety of BBC television shows.

This is what they told us:

Is internet dating a good way to meet people?
Jamie Smart: It's great to get you interacting, and meeting people outside your social network. It can work especially well if you are good with written words. If you're not, think of it as a starting point, and get on the phone or in person as quickly as possible to open the maximum number of communication channels. Remember that, face-to-face, 7 per cent of communication is words, 34 per cent voice, tone and pace, and 59 per cent body language.

Sarah Whittaker: Internet dating is an excellent way to focus your search for a partner – I met my husband through the *Guardian*'s Soulmates, and only wish it had been online back then.

Max Blumberg: It increases choice, and the more choice you have, the better the chance of meeting someone you're going to be happy with.

How can we create an appealing online profile?
JS: For men it's important to sound self-assured. Don't apologise for yourself. Women like profiles which sound confident. But don't confuse this with arrogance – a sign of low self-esteem.

And don't set impossible standards. If your date has to be a 6-foot-tall blonde Greek sky-diving novelist, you are unlikely to get responses and are setting out not to find love.

MB: We consider ourselves to be quite sophisticated, but the way people choose partners has changed little since thousands of years ago, when men chose women based primarily on their physical appearance and women looked for good providers.

How does this help the modern internet dater? Well, if you

are female, on top of your interests, remember to mention your attractive, caring and youthful attributes.

Men should emphasise intelligence, kindness, sensitivity, confidence, a sense of humour, a wide range of interests, openness to new experiences and an ability to socialise – all attractive attributes to women.

Is email a good way of establishing a relationship?

JS: With email you're not getting the whole story – that is why people use emoticons. In the old days, however, people used to woo each other with letters, so modern technology combined with old-fashioned literary courtship is not a bad combination.

MB: Yes, in the early stages. But there are many cues that cannot be assessed via email, such as whether the eyes smile at the same time as the mouth – telling you if a person is genuine. But you can certainly sense if someone's values and interests are similar to yours, although when you meet them, you still need to check whether their behaviour matches what they say.

Is attraction or love 'chemical'? To be found randomly, rather than by something as 'methodical' as internet dating?

SW: Hormones play a part in attraction, but by being 'methodical' in our search we will at least be meeting someone who shares our values, interests and lifestyle.

JS: Love is a complex interaction. It's chemical in that we are stimulated by smell or the sound of someone's voice and because people sometimes form relationships to resolve troubles they had with their parents. Unfortunately this can lead us into recurring bad relationships, so a bit of 'methodical' sifting out of people who are bad for us when internet dating is no bad thing.

Attraction is different for men and women. Men are visually driven, while women are driven only 30 per cent by looks and 70 per cent by other factors. For women a man's status is often more important than his looks; the higher his status, the more attractive he is. An episode of the TV show *Mrs Merton* illustrated this: she was interviewing Paul Daniels and his wife Debbie McGee. Mrs Merton asked McGee: 'What first attracted you to short, balding millionaire Paul Daniels?' She then turned to Paul Daniels and said, 'What first attracted you to slim, blonde 20-year-old Debbie McGee?'

Now nobody will sign up to the notion that they are so shallow as to be just after money or looks, but if the rock stars, millionaires and football players are going out with supermodels then status and looks are clearly factors.

MB: If you think about it, most relationships in most cultures – including ours – are the result of introductions made by friends, family, and work colleagues. And if they cannot introduce us to a 'chemical' match, we might well settle for a more pragmatic relationship instead. Pragmatic relationships have been shown to last longer and be more satisfying than 'chemical' relationships anyway.

What should people expect from internet dating?
SW: Expect to have fun, meet interesting people, make new friends and discover great restaurants and bars. Don't expect to find someone to make you whole or fix your past problems – that's *your* job.

MB: Women: If you have an attractive photo, expect approaches from every man that sees it. Watch out for partnered men on dating sites; suspect anybody who can't speak to you on weekends.

Men: You are far more likely to get responses by making the approach than by sitting back and waiting for it. If you have written your profile showing yourself to be an intelligent, kind and interesting guy, you should get good responses. A photograph is important, not because women are just wanting good looks, but because women are able to visually judge personality rather well.

Why do some people feel uncomfortable dating? Is there anything they can do to improve this?

SW: Lack of self-confidence is incredibly common. I've worked with people who feel suffocated by their social mask, sometimes people you would never think lacked confidence. It seems obvious – but if you like yourself, others will mostly like you too.

JS: It's a vicious circle. If social situations make you tense and uptight it's hard to connect with people, so you become tenser – but you can change this. Often people do this by drinking, but if you would like to do this without drugs, there is a way. In NLP we call it state management. You check the state you're in, by being aware of the feelings in your body, your thoughts and words. You then direct your mind to the state you would like to be in.

It's hard to believe that you can change. But we all know people who come into a room, and take the mood down – and the opposite type of person, who lifts the mood. The difference between them is their internal state: their 'vibe', as hippies used to call it. You can change your 'vibe' if you want – and this can help you with dating.

How can you make others feel relaxed in your presence?

SW: By being truly yourself. If you express genuine kindness and warmth, and show a real interest in your date, this will be enough to relax them.

JS: Most obviously it helps if you are relaxed yourself – it's unlikely that other people will feel relaxed if you aren't. There are techniques that you can use to help other people feel at ease with you, like matching their body posture.

Another way to relax people is to establish a rapport with them. A simple way of doing this is to describe the current situation. Maybe at the beginning of a first date you might talk about how you are meeting: 'It's Friday night, this is the first time we've met, so we can enjoy getting to know each other.' It may seem obvious and even trite but you'll see that they are nodding their head and getting into rapport with you. They are starting to feel safe, and relax. Now look out for remarks that get confirmation, and see that as a clue for a positive direction to go in. This is the opposite of the daters who go into monologues about a shooting weekend on a date with someone who hates guns – they certainly won't feel safe and relaxed with you if you keep talking about them.

MB: Don't focus only on yourself, but ask questions about them (a balance is important – don't make it sound like an interrogation!). Keep the conversation light initially.

Clothes, appearance: are they important?
SW: It doesn't matter what you wear, as long as you're comfortable and wholesome-looking. Try to deal with any off-putting physical stuff like bad breath or greasy hair before you go dating. But airbrushed perfection is not the goal – if you feel happy and relaxed, you'll glow, whatever physical good or bad points you are blessed with.

JS: Overall, I'd say do the best with what you have. We've talked about men being more visually orientated than women. But that doesn't mean that men don't need to pay any attention to their appearance. If a guy looks like George Clooney, he can turn up in a boiler suit and do OK, but if he looked more stylish, he'd do better.

You can pick up on clothing clues before you meet someone. For example, if you know that a woman likes shoes (she says so in her profile, or in conversation), then she may well take notice of what shoes you are wearing. And clothes give clues to a man's status – which is important to women.

MB: Women: men often put women into two camps upon first meeting them – short-term fling or long-term prospect. As a woman, dressing very sexy on the first date may put you into the first group. This is fine if it is what you are looking for. If it is not, you may want to dress slightly more conservatively.

Men: although women do not categorise men in this way (women make no distinction between short-term and long-term prospects), they can – and do – read a lot about you from your clothing (if nothing else, how much you tried to impress them!). Dress smart, especially for initial dates.

Are alcohol/drugs a good way to help a date move along?

JS: Drink can help you feel more confident, but at the same time it's not good for decision making and often leads you in directions you wouldn't want to go.

If you feel you can use drink or drugs safely, that's a choice. But I would suggest a different approach. There are ways to raise your confidence naturally – the state changing exercise I mentioned earlier, for example.

SW: If you *have* to consume alcohol or drugs in order to relax and have fun, then something's wrong. I've worked with many people who feel inadequate and under-confident when they go out to bars and clubs – they feel compelled to drink or use cocaine to relax. I offer them alternatives, and once they find they are not reliant on drugs to have a good time, they enjoy themselves even more.

MB: Women are unlikely to be impressed by a man who needs substance assistance – it indicates a lack of confidence. Men, as ever, are less likely to be fussy, and are more likely to view a woman who is high or drunk as an easier sexual prospect.

How can we communicate more positively when we are dating?

SW: It's amazing how many people run themselves down all the time, saying to me 'I'm just crap at relationships'. People even do it in their online profiles, where it screams low self-esteem, rather than self-deprecating wit.

This low self-esteem comes across as negative when we are dating. I worked with an extremely pretty woman in her 20s, who would put men off by constantly putting herself down. But once she recognised what she was doing, and acknowledged her good points, her ability to receive love skyrocketed.

JS: If you are off in your head, thinking about something else – tomorrow, next week, or what might happen later in the evening – you are not connecting. If you are telling a story, but don't pay attention to the response, then you won't know if you're having the effect you want. It's not communication, just running off at the mouth. I know someone who, when he gets nervous, starts to talk about cars – not good on a date – unless she's a Formula One driver. If he could just listen and get into the present, he'd see the effect he is having.

Both sexes need to pay closer attention to their dates. Men need to look out for signals that women are giving them. Often they will be on a date, and the woman is signalling like mad that she's interested in them, by playing with her hair, fiddling with her clothes, licking her lips, and they won't pick up on it. Sometimes a woman can feel she's been blatantly flirting, and be stunned that a man has not picked up on her signals or just assume that he is not interested.

The opposite of this are 'clumsy' men who can't read the signals that a woman is not interested, but simply assume she is.

Unfortunately, women leave it up to men to pick up on the signals, so it's important for them to look and listen, so wires don't get crossed. Turn off the internal monologue in your head and be observant, watch and listen.

What is flirting?
SW: Grown-up playing.

JS: Milan Kundera defined it as 'offering the *possibility* of sexual contact, without making any promises'. It's a ritual we go through to prepare us for intimacy or sex. Women tend to be more dialled into it than men, schooled in flirting through romantic films, books and stories.

Men need to get on board more – talk more about things that she's interested in. It means they can be sexual without being lewd – flirting and sex don't live in different realms. Communicate to a woman that you are sexual without being blatant.

MB: It's the act of letting someone know that you fancy them. Don't overdo it, but a subtle compliment here and there will get the message across. No compliments or sexy body language at all usually means the other person is not interested.

Isn't it manipulative to develop techniques for flirting and seduction?
JS: If manipulation is off the cards, then no more make-up, no more

perfume. Looking your best is manipulation, but it's also respectful of the other person, showing them that you value them.

The flirting ritual is 'romantic theatre'. Think about all the clichés associated with 'romance' – princes 'saving you' (and if you read some women's profiles online they use these clichés) and so on. Flirting and courtship rituals are all about creating the sense of romance. Is that honest? Well, as long as the intent is honest it is. Trying to make someone fall in love with you to have a one-night stand – that's dishonest. There are techniques which will make people feel more at ease in your presence. These are tools, like a knife – you can use a knife to make a meal, or to stab someone. Don't question the knife, question your ethics.

MB: If you learn techniques and use them to break hearts, I would say that is manipulative. It is up to your personal morals whether you would do this.

Some daters make instant decisions about compatibility when they meet people for a date. Is this 'chemistry' or simply 'blind' blind dating?
MB: Relationship research has shown time and again that chemistry, no matter how wonderful it feels, is no great predictor of relationship success. Of course chemistry is a critical factor, but it is not enough to ensure compatibility or guarantee relationship satisfaction. Satisfaction also depends on a number of other factors, such as compatible lifestyles and the ability to communicate well. These take time to discover in another person. So take time getting to know someone and enjoy the journey for its own sake without putting too much pressure on the outcome, especially in the early stages of a relationship.

SW: Sadly, we all have a tendency to make up our minds about people pretty instantly – but try to look beyond initial appearance.

Does your date have a good heart in that bad suit? Gut feelings can be powerful indicators, though, so if you're sure that you're not just being picky to avoid risking intimacy, trust your feelings.

JS: The 'chemistry' factor is important. But it's equally true that people find themselves attracted to friends they have known for a period of time. It's important to give time to discover your date – otherwise what would be the point of it, you might as well just have a two-minute meeting – so don't put pressure on the thunderbolt to strike.

'Chemistry' is all kinds of things – energy, smell, rhythm, etc. But true communication can't be reliably established in the first 30 seconds. Maybe your instinct is right, but don't rely on it. People win the lottery, but it's hardly a sensible investment strategy. And we all know that you can have an instant attraction to someone who won't be a long-term partner.

Internet dating can be fast. People can get involved quickly, and jump off quickly in the knowledge that they can go back online in search of new people. Often their profiles say they want commitment, but in practice they don't.
SW: Some people say they keep ending up with commitment-phobes – but end up realising that they are subconsciously *choosing* emotionally unavailable partners. Perhaps it's so that they don't have to deal with their own fear of commitment, or in order to re-play familiar family patterns, or maybe it's because of feelings that they don't deserve to be loved.

I see many men with this problem, and – despite what women think – it can be very distressing to them. Often, they know they have a tendency to run out on good women to avoid relationships. It can lead to serious self-esteem problems, or to unhappy serial dating, and a trail of broken hearts. But it doesn't have to end up this way. People can change.

MB: It's mostly men who say they want commitment because they know women usually want to hear this (although younger women are becoming less demanding of commitment). How can you test for true commitment? Usually this will show in a person's general ethics and morals in areas even unrelated to dating because people are seldom moral in one area and immoral in another – morality tends to be consistent. In other words, if they lie about their job, they were probably lying about their commitment to you too.

Putting yourself on display on an internet site opens you to rejection – from not getting any interest, or replies to your mails, to never getting beyond the first date. Are there strategies to cope with this?

MB: For some, attracting others is a natural skill or ability; others need to learn to make the most of themselves. The key is that 'attractiveness' can be learned. This doesn't mean that you can make the exact person you want fall for you, but it does mean that you can learn how to make the most of yourself so that you can get the attention you deserve. There are coaches who can teach you how to become a good conversationalist, how to write dating profiles that attract attention, and how to make the most of your looks no matter what your shape or size – if makeovers are good enough for Brad and Britney, they are good enough for the rest of us! If you have fears about dating, there are counsellors who can assist with this.

In other words, with a bit of effort and perhaps some outside help, no one need experience the rejection of not getting interest from their profile or getting beyond the first date.

JS: Remember it's a numbers game. Don't focus on one person on a website, email 50, and chat to 20.

If you start feeling the weight of rejection, think about the people in your life who do love you. Fear of rejection takes us back to tribal times, when being banished really was a fate worse than death. Now, obviously it is not.

To prove that, try what I call the 'Pizza Walk'. Visit some shops and make absurd requests. Ask McDonald's for a pizza, a hardware shop for lingerie, an electrical shop for flowers. You see how little there is to fear in rejection, and that it's not about you.

SW: No one likes rejection. However, an internet dating rejection need not be something to take too personally – after all, there are people who don't appeal to you, who you will 'reject'. But if rejection, or fear of rejection, is getting you down, it may be that a past traumatic rejection is making you particularly sensitive to feeling unwanted. I see people with problems like this, and you can be de-sensitised to rejection so that you can take it in your stride.

Some people go online in order to feel wanted, or gauge their attractiveness. Is this wise?
MB: There are no definite rights or wrongs because everyone is so different. I believe that most of us know our attractiveness without needing to go and check it online. If we are going online because we cannot attract people offline, we are likely to be setting ourselves up for failure because, sooner or later, the relationship is likely to move to the real world and our original offline problems are likely to recur.

A better strategy would be to gain insight into why we find relationships difficult in general, deal with these issues by seeking out help and advice, and only then enter the world of online dating. Then when you do meet others and there is mutual attraction, you'll be in a better position to create something meaningful.

SW: If this is you, ask yourself what you can do to boost your inner self-confidence – are you feeling unsure of your own worth? If so, dating is not the answer.

JS: Humans have a need to feel important. If your self-esteem is low and it works for you to go online and see that there are people out there who are interested, go for it. But remember the more you love yourself, the more other people will love you.

Internet dating can create a lot of initial excitement. How do you keep things going?

SW: It's normal for an initially exciting and intense relationship to develop into something more laid-back and chilled. However, taking your partner for granted is a short-cut back to singledom.

JS: Explore. Treat the other person like your secret lover.

MB: It's no different with non-internet dating. Relationships are living things. They need to be fed, watered and nurtured in order to grow and thrive. You can't just leave them to their own de- vices and expect them to develop into something meaningful. So the usual rules for successful relationships apply. Try new things with each other, take time to learn each other's interests, woo each other all over again periodically like it was your first date (even if this feels silly!), and make time to talk about the relation- ship periodically (yes men, this includes you!).

For more information about Sarah Whittaker visit www.phoenix homeopathy.com.

For more information about Jamie Smart, and free tips on how you can use NLP to improve the results you get, visit www.saladltd.co.uk.

Chapter 10

A DATE WITH THE FUTURE

Is Online Dating Here to Stay?

In less than a decade internet dating has changed the way we meet our potential partners. The ease and speed of cyberdating has left dating agencies and lonely hearts columns floundering in its wake. But is internet dating simply the latest fad, or is it the future?

'It's here to stay', insists Fiona Maclean from My UK Date, 'because it suits the way we live now. In the 1950s, people would meet and marry after school or college and their relationships used to be for life. Now we travel, move city, and change partners so often that we need a quick, easy way to meet new people. The more mobile we become, the more we will use the internet to find friends and romance.'

Samantha Bedford, UK MD at Match, agrees: 'In our recent survey we discovered that with people's busy, ever-changing, energy-depleting lifestyles they simply don't have time to wait for Cupid's intervention. Modern daters use the internet to carry out a considered and dedicated search. Some people are so focused that they create "dating dossiers", and arrange "date-meets" with friends where they award points to the best and worst candidates. It's a completely different way of searching for love than in previous generations.'

What will we tell the grandchildren?

So internet dating reflects our changing lifestyles. But for some the pace of change is at odds with their 'traditional' ideas of romance. They feel uneasy about revealing to friends and family that they found their new boyfriend or girlfriend on a computer screen. As one dater put it: 'What will we tell the grandchildren?'

'Many of us feel our pride is hurt by having to resort to technology', says psychotherapist Albyn Hall. 'Just look at the number of online profiles which state: "I can't believe I'm doing this." This is particularly true for women, who are primed to be the chosen objects of desire. They don't want to be reminded that they are being selected via machine, and not across a crowded room.'

But, wounded pride or not, over two-thirds of UK singles who are looking for love do so on the internet. And while some keep it secret, others are outspoken enthusiasts. 'In the last three years online dating has undergone something of a revolution', says Simon Dale, co-founder of Snog London. 'Where once it had a stigma, now it's becoming cool, with friends and colleagues sharing dating experiences over the water cooler.'

The net widens

Cyberdating was born during the baby steps of the information revolution, and many experts believe that as technology develops, so will internet dating: 'In the next two years broadband will become the norm', says Fiona Maclean. 'Dating sites will offer video chat, as an alternative to text chat.'

'But the big change', says Maclean, 'will be mobile technology. Text flirting is already popular on younger sites like Date the UK. Soon you will be able to send profiles and pictures to people's mobiles – rather than just text flirts. As WAP becomes faster and less fiddly, sites will offer dating on the move. So you might be out in the centre of London, and via your mobile, ask your dating site if there is someone else in London who fits your search criteria. If there is, you send them a text. They look at your profile via their phone, and if they are free, you could arrange to meet.'

What is clear is that as technology changes, dating changes; but how much and how quickly is impossible to know. As one dating futurologist puts it, 'Maybe in 20 years' time we will all be wearing silver suits while internet dating and sending our robots out on the first date to avoid the embarrassing tricky first moments.'

Internet dating the old-fashioned way

But for some people, all these extra bells and whistles may not be what they want. 'Many daters prefer the written word to the intrusion of a webcam', says internet dating expert Jill Duffield. 'We've seen how it takes time for a relationship to progress from email to the phone. Email gives people anonymity, flexibility and safety – a webcam means you have to reveal yourself immediately.'

And many sites realise that the dating experience is not automatically improved by adding webcams, with many daters looking for a more 'human' experience. Some, like Snog London, list a direct phone number to the office, giving a sense of the people behind the scenes. Others have online personas. 'People want to find the human element to internet dating', says Maclean. 'So as sites develop, they will add personal touches by having "reps". A bit like holiday reps, who join in discussions on the forums, email people who need technical help, and send out newsletters. "Emma" is our human face on My UK Date.'

'The more human internet dating seems, the easier it is to

do', agrees Hall. 'Nobody feels romantic about computers – but we have a romantic idea about who is behind them. It may have been around for only a decade, but there's a 'courtship ritual' to internet dating: the approach, the first email, the first phone call, the date – people understand this. I have a friend who started dating and gave out her mobile phone number too soon – her suitor was unhappy, because she'd broken e-courting etiquette.'

'If dating starts to feel like a Playstation,' Hall continues, 'there may be a backlash. People are basically romantic, they have all kinds of fantasies about who, and how, they will meet. When you internet date from your home PC, you can sit in your study with a glass of wine, listening to Billie Holiday and imagining the tall, dark handsome stranger at the end of your broadband. But an instant mobile-phone date? Do you really want to find your match served up via a flashing facia which tweets out silly ring tones?'

'Of course, there are different experiences for different generations', adds Hall. 'So the over-30s will feel more at home with "old-style" websites, while younger people are happy with instant technology. And as things get even faster in the future, no doubt people will look back to our times as terribly quaint: "My gran met my grandfather on the internet, and they waited *four weeks* before they got together."'

Losing site?

With over 800 internet dating sites in the UK alone, and around a hundred new sites joining the fray each year, can we expect the number to increase to thousands in the future?

Most experts think that McDating megasites, such as Udate and Match, are here to stay. But they also agree that there's not much room left for new sites in this market. The boom, according to Snog London's Simon Dale, will be in 'smaller "niche" sites which cater to personal interests and lifestyle choices – religious beliefs, education, or sexual orientation'.

It's hard to believe that we'll all be Googling tadpolelovers.com or origamidating.net in the future. But there is good reason to believe we will. Research shows that most people use internet dating to find 'people like us'. Niche sites tap into this: 'opposites attract' is a charming romantic cliché, but in practice daters are looking for partners of a similar income, age, education and social status. Niche sites save us from having to sift through thousands of people who don't share our values and ideas.

Newspapers are ideally placed to exploit the idea of niche dating. A newspaper defines so much about its reader: social group, politics, education and aspirations. The *Guardian*'s online Soulmates is a perfect example of this: daters know the 'type' of person they will find there. So we can expect more newspapers to create dating sites in the future.

Another buzzword for the dating sites will be 'communities'. Rather than just offering vanilla dating, they will include places where you can chat and make friends. Discussion forums – like the one on Love and Friends – will be places where people can get to know each other away from the dating area, giving the site a community feel. 'Forums create "brand loyalty"', says Fiona Maclean. 'They keep people associated with the site even when they have met people. So if they break up in the future, they will come back to the place that matched them in the first place.'

'Sites will definitely offer a more expansive service', says Snog London's Dale. 'Not just providing dating partner searches, but adding extra depth. They will be like one-stop-shops for everything. I wouldn't be surprised if in five or ten years' time, most people met online.'

This all-round service will come into its own on city-specific sites. These will be as much about socialising as they are about dating. Snog London caters for romance in the metropolis, but visit the discussion forum and you'll find that many of the regulars use it as much to boost their social life as they do to find partners. Forum messages referring to Snog London simply as a dating site are met with a barrage of ripostes informing them that the site is 'so much more than just dating'. So how long before there is a MeetManchester.com or a DateDerby.net?

New sites

So what will these future niche sites be like? In addition to 'branded' sites, affiliated to newspapers and magazines, there will also be sites for *FHM*-style lads and ladettes. Shagaholic.com is an example of this type of site, aimed at feisty women who don't like the hardcore element of the sex sites, but want to go out and have 'fun'. Faceparty is another example of a site which is more about finding sex than finding a lifetime partner.

As well as the 'sex posing as dating' sites, there will be 'dating posing as lifestyle' sites. An example of this is lavalife.com, which is aimed at people who think they are too good to be on a dating site – well-educated, good-looking, wealthy people, who actually want to use dating sites, but still can't believe they have to.

The human touch

But will there be a point at which people no longer accept being driven by technology, and start to rebel? Will this lead to 'human contact' being integrated onto sites? Singles event management is fast becoming a vital ingredient of the bigger dating sites as they recognise the value of the Bridget Jones pound. Match has successfully married its online service to its offline business of organising events.

Singles holidays, book clubs (already available on Love and Friends) and dating events are all being added to dating sites. 'Speed-dating is a great complement to online dating', says Samantha Bedford of Match. 'Over the last eighteen months it has taken off in a big way. You can go to any small UK city and there'll be a speed-dating event. People like to have an environment to meet in which is not a conventional date to make it more human. People who go along expect to have a fun evening – not to find The One. You've got local pubs organising their own speed-dating events. I can see it becoming like the pub quiz. A weekly event at your local that's always there.'

How many frogs?

Internet dating is the modern way to find love. If you are determined and persistent, eventually you will find what you are looking for. 'Think about internet dating as a romantic version of shopping', says Albyn Hall. 'Keep browsing, try a few out, and eventually you'll find the right fit.'

'Twinkle' from Love and Friends is the supreme example of the modern internet dater. She decided to 'try out' every man who emailed her. 'After 149 dates with different men, it worked', she says. 'And I'm still dating him. He was number 17.'

Twinkle's story is a parable for the internet dating world. Like the modern shopper or the frog-kissing princess, keep at it, and eventually your prince (or princess) will appear.

What internet dating has done for me

❝Internet dating has meant an opportunity to meet like-minded people without having to trail bars, join book clubs and sign up to evening classes in ceramics and flower-arranging. I have met some fantastic people who I doubt I would have met in 'real life'. I've had some great nights out and the odd disastrous date to relate to friends.❞

Dan, journalist, 31

❝My wife died from cancer two years ago leaving me to bring up our two young daughters. I joined a dating site as a 'newly single parent' which I thought would put people off – but I was inundated with replies and offers to meet up. Now I go out every Saturday night – either with potential dates or with my new 'allies'. I'm happy and my daughters think it's great – they even tell me what to wear.❞

Clive, IT sales, 45

❝Internet dating has given me some of the most memorable experiences of my life at a time when I wasn't up to going out to bars and clubs but was quite happy to 'dabble' from home in my pyjamas. It can be a great way to get back in the saddle after falling off the horse of relationships when your self-confidence is at an all-time low.❞

Sarah, investment banker, 33

❝The beauty of internet dating is you can do it at your own pace from the comfort of your own home without having to leave the house. I have had manic, full-on phases where I've contacted loads of men and gone on several dates in one week. But I've also had quiet periods where I hardly log on at all and only react if a really good email comes in. Basically it's a fantastic extra 'tool' you can employ as and when you want to.❞

Sarah, sales executive, 31

❝Most of my friends have met their girlfriends online and are in relationships to this day. So to say it works would be somewhat of an understatement.❞

Mary, publisher, 37

❝What has internet dating given me? An encyclopaedic knowledge of London pubs. I made it my duty to meet every new date in a different pub – of her suggestion. That way, even if the date's a little dull, I get to know a new pub. But seriously, no date is a waste of time – on a couple of occasions where we've not 'clicked', I've introduced the woman to one of my friends – one couple is still together now.❞

Simon, retail manager, 39

❝When all my friends were coupling up and having babies, internet dating gave me an 'alternative' social life. Suddenly I had a stream of men waiting in the wings who I could 'bring in to land' when the fancy took me. Some dates were good, some were bad, but so far I've had a couple of significant relationships and made several life-long friends.❞

Carol, social worker, 43

❝Even if I haven't yet met the love of my life I've met some really interesting people – two who became short-term boyfriends, one who gave me really useful career advice, another who found me my flat, and countless friends. I joined a dating site one week after the end of a disastrous relationship and within days I'd got over 200 emails. I went on 40 dates in a six-month period and in that time only met one person I would class as dull. As long as you're quite selective and ring people first – it's a great way of meeting new people.❞

Sarah, lawyer, 48

&&*I met the great David, as I call him, and two years of the most intense, passionate and loving relationship followed. A truly life-enhancing relationship.* &&

Elaine, writer, 35

&&*When Richard showed up – not my type at all from his photo – initially I ignored him, but his emails were so funny and so persistent that eventually I 'caved in' and we arranged to meet. Maybe because my expectations were so low, I was utterly relaxed on our first date and we ended up chatting till 4 a.m. The next day I told my by now sceptical work mates I'd met my 'future husband'. We got married exactly one year to the day.* &&

Petra, marketing executive, 37

INDEX